Gwenda Sloane : The Strangest Killer

Nathaniel Nixon

Published by Trellis Publishing, 2021.

While every precaution has been taken in the preparation of this book, the publisher assumes no responsibility for errors or omissions, or for damages resulting from the use of the information contained herein.

GWENDA SLOANE : THE STRANGEST KILLER

First edition. July 12, 2021.

Copyright © 2021 Nathaniel Nixon.

ISBN: 979-8224487318

Written by Nathaniel Nixon.

Gwenda Sloane :

The Strangest Killer

Nathaniel Nixon

Gwenda Sloane

Gwenda Sloane doesn't fit the typical mold of a murderer. We often think of murderers as displaying inconsistent behavior and having alternate motives to their actions. Many times, murderers show a history of crime and recklessness. Gwenda Sloane simply doesn't fit these criteria.

In crimes that have taken place over the previous decade, the murder committed by Gwenda Sloane didn't garner as much attention as some others of a similar time period. This is partly due to the location of the murder and the lack of international media attention with it. If this story had taken place in the United States of America, this would have undoubtedly been one of the biggest stories from anywhere in the nation. The lack of international media attention around the case doesn't make the crime any less chaotic. This crime was one of unimaginable circumstance and truly heartless actions. The murder committed by Gwenda Sloane is a prime example of how the most innocent of faces can commit truly heinous crimes.

Gwenda Leigh Sloane was born in New Zealand in 1969. Her early life is most largely unknown. According to court documents, she lived an ordinary childhood while facing an average amount of obstacles. The most known fact of her childhood was her lack of social skills. This was not to say that she was bullied or in any sort of depression, but that she simply delayed in social skills with regard to making friends and fitting in. Sloane spoke little of her childhood to anyone that she formed relationships with. To most anyone in connection with the case or around Sloane, they knew little of what her life was really like early on. For all intents and purposes, she ultimately graduated from high school in a respectable fashion.

Gwenda settled into an area on the North Island of New Zealand, in the Bay of Plenty Region known as Rotorua. This area is sparsely populated. Each resident here enjoys a reasonable amount of privacy. New Zealand itself, however, is a very dense country that is known for a modest standard of living. Gwenda Sloane was able to settle into this area of North Island reasonably easily. Most everyone who came to knew her had known her to be here her whole life. This is where the story of Gwenda Sloane truly starts.

Gwenda was a quiet and unassuming individual. She was a short woman who kept to herself. She was slightly overweight, with a chubby face that seemed truly innocent and collected. Her appearance was not at all intimidating or standoffish; it was actually quite inviting and warm.

This appearance is perhaps why she was able to form trusting and sincere relationships with those who came in to contact with her. Most anyone would assume only the best about Gwenda. She had provided absolutely no reason to not be trusted or to think that she could have anything but the best intentions in her heart. This way of thinking about Gwenda would soon be proven wrong.

Michelle Hoffman-Tamm had lived a much more organized and typical life. She settled in Rotorua and started the typical family life. She married and had children. For almost 15 years, she lived this life. To all that knew her, she was a happy and attempting mother and wife to her children and husband.

She soon would realize that her route to happiness did not lie in this typical lifestyle. She would divorce her husband, and soon move in with her female partner. This change in lifestyle came as a shock to all who knew her, however, was supported by her family and friends.

Michelle Hoffman-Tamm lived with her partner, Inoi Samuels, for over 15 years. The couple had a serious relationship and appeared happy to most anyone that was around them. They didn't share a monogamous relationship, but enjoyed trust and happiness with each other for the duration of their relationship.

From the time that Michelle Hoffman-Tamm had begun her initial marriage to her husband, she had formed several relationships with other women. Of these relationships, one seemed to stand out as the closest. Michelle Hoffman-Tamm formed an intense personal relationship with Gwenda Sloane.

Gwenda was frequently round the Hoffman-Tamm family. In fact, Michelle's daughter, Monique, had formed such a close relationship with Gwenda that she called her "Aunty." Gwenda was frequently at family events and had a deep involvement with her children.

Michelle and Gwenda had a friendship that would span roughly 20 years. Throughout this time, they shared a deep sexual bond and formed a trust with each other that rivaled most marriages. Michelle's friends and family knew of the deep bond and connection that the pair shared. While it was not a typical relationship, it seemed to be an ultimately healthy and solid relationship that most everyone accepted.

On November 7, 2012, everything would change in a drastic and unforgettable fashion. Michelle Hoffman-Tamm, who was still living with her partner Inoi Samuels, would leave their home in the late afternoon. She left on her bike, and gave no indication of where she was going. The events that would unfold are gruesome and heartbreaking.

When a couple of days went by and no one had heard from Michelle, her family filed a missing person's report to the Rotorua police department. She had not returned text messages or phone calls from anyone, not even her children or partner. Most everyone knew that something was wrong. She was never the type of woman to leave her family in the dark to her whereabouts.

As days turned to weeks, many people around the family began to question if Michelle was safe. While some feared the worst, there were numerous family members who felt like she may have possibly ran-off with a new lover. Police asked all of those who were close to Michelle if they had any recollection of the events around her disappearance. All that anyone truly knew was that on November 7th, she had left her home on a bike and had not been seen since. Gwenda was contacted many times, however she claimed that she hadn't heard from her and didn't see her on November 7th. Initially, no one would suspect that

Gwenda had anything to do with her disappearance. After all, she was like a second mother to Michelle's children. She had no criminal record and seemed to be the trustworthy, honest, and sincere woman that was a constant for the entire family.

After more than two weeks, investigators caught a huge break in the case. After routine questioning, one of those being interrogated finally spoke as to what had happened. This person led police to the body. When police arrived on scene, they learned that the identity of the body was none other than Michelle Hoffman-Tamm. With the tragic news that would rock an entire community and the Hoffman-Tamm family, their worst fears that Michelle may be dead had been proven true. On November 23, 2012, just off of Highway 38 near Murupara, New Zealand, Michelle Hoffman-Tamm had officially been found. It was apparent that she had been deceased for several weeks. But who finally had come forward and provided the evidence as to what had happened to Michelle? The answer to that question was one of the last people that anyone would have ultimately suspected. It was none other than Gwenda Sloane.

Throughout the investigation, police had contacted and questioned most anyone who knew Michelle. Those who had frequent contact with Michelle, such as Gwenda, her children, and Inoi, were contacted regularly. Police knew that it was likely that one of them knew more than what they were offering to tell. Gwenda stood out to police for many reasons.

Gwenda Sloane had a long and documented relationship with Michelle. It was odd to police, however, that the couple had not lived together. Police found it hard to grasp that someone who was so close to Michelle's family was not an official "partner" of Michelle. Also, police noted that several within the family spoke of how distant Gwenda had become since the disappearance of Michelle. This in itself is not all too suspicious, but it was odd that someone that was so close to others in the family would not be there for them in such a time of need.

On November 22, police found Gwenda to question her once more. It was at this time that she came clean with everything that had happened. She would then lead them to the body of Michelle Hoffman-Tamm. Police readily admitted that without this confession, it was extremely unlikely they would have found the body in such a secluded, well-hidden area. The story that Gwenda would go to tell investigators is so unimaginable that it would lead many to leave the courtroom when it was being told. For someone who cared so deeply for another to commit this type of murder is hard to grasp. The events of November 7th and the following days are truly evil.

The following recollection of events is the exact confession that Gwenda Sloane, herself, had told police. She did little to hold back details as to specifics on what had happened. Upon examination of the body, police were able to piece together an even more extreme scenario that painted a vivid picture of what truly happened to Michelle Hoffman-Tamm.

The Murder

Just before 11:00 P.M. Gwenda Sloane was sitting comfortably in her home. She had been communicating with Michelle often throughout the day, as was the case most each and every day. At 11:00 P.M. Sloane sent Hoffman-Tamm a provocative text message.

"Hello my little monkey. Want to have some fun," the message read.

Looking back at phone records, this was the last text message that was sent from Sloane to Hoffman-Tamm. Michelle responded simply by stating she was on her way. This would be the last communication between them through the phone. Records also indicate that this sort of communication was not at all 'out of the blue'. The pair frequently exchanged similar text messages that spanned for years. Michelle likely thought little more of this text message than an innocent sexual rendezvous between the two.

Within a matter of minutes, Michelle left her home by bicycle and headed off to Gwenda's house. She made no statements as to where she was going. Being as this was a common procedure for her, she surely wouldn't have been thinking that she needed to explain where she was going.

Michelle headed straight for Gwenda's home. When she arrived, the pair planned to make a similar night together as they had frequently done in the past. The pair went to a local store and bought over 3 dozen cans of beer. According to the investigation, it was common for store employees to see the pair come in and purchase large amounts of alcohol. After purchasing their beer, they headed back to Gwenda's home and began their night.

According to Gwenda, the couple had about 10 beers that evening before they slept together. They had one of their typical sexual escapades in Gwenda's bedroom. When they had finished, they returned back to the living room where they continued to drink heavily.

Up until this point, everything was completely normal for what they had typically done. At least twice per month, the pair had enjoyed nights of a similar fashion. According to Gwenda, the couple had partaken in this sort of evening hundreds of times over the previous 20 years. If the night had continued as it normally had, Michelle would have woken up early to go back to her home. The couple would have enjoyed a heavy night of drinking and sexual encounters as they saw fit. Instead, Gwenda decided to change the routine.

The most disputed part of the entire murder case was the reason that Gwenda gave for her outrage. The motive that she gave for her killing of Michelle was simply outrageous. The reason she gave for her decision is the single fact that would grab headline all over New Zealand and the eastern world. Many believe that there is much more to the crime than the reason that Gwenda provided, however no one will ever know unless Gwenda herself speaks more on the topic.

After a heavy evening of drinking, there is no doubt that judgements had been impaired on both sides. Each of the women were obviously heavily intoxicated at the time of the crime. At some point in the evening, after the two had already had sex and had at least 30 beers between them, Gwenda claims that she, herself, just snapped.

Gwenda launched an extremely hostile attack on Michelle. She claims that she rushed her intensely and hit her over the head with a kitchen drawer. She then chose two large knives to inflict the fatal wounds.

Gwenda Sloane stabbed Michelle Hoffman-Tamm an unprecedented 33 times. The larger of the two knives that she used was 4.5 centimeters wide while the other was just over 1 centimeter.

Police estimate that 25 of the 33 stab wounds found on Michelle's body had likely happened after she was already dead. In addition to the 33 stab wounds, Michelle also had blunt force trauma to her head, likely as a result of the kitchen drawer being broken over her head. She had several teeth that had been knocked out in addition to several bruises and lacerations on her scalp.

The majority of the stab wounds were to the chest and the back. Gwenda Sloane claims that she initially stabbed her in the chest after she had hit her across the head with the drawer. She continued to stab her in the chest until she rolled over just after the attack had begun.

The most disturbing part of the case was the condition of the body upon police finding it in the ditch. Gwenda had mutilated Michelle's body after she was already deceased. She had made several full penetration cuts to her face from her mouth to her ears and eyes. She had even severed her nose and ears off. Police found Michelle's ears in her own mouth.

The mutilation is what sets this case apart from a typical murder. To prosecutors, this shows a true malice and viciousness to the crime that can only be attributed to someone who truly wanted to eradicate someone. They claim that she wanted to embarrass Michelle beyond just ending her life. It was clear to prosecutors that Gwenda was extremely angry about something. She made it a point to get her agenda across.

After Gwenda had finished with her attack on Michelle, she readily admits that her next move was to head back to the living room and finish the beers that they had bought. The entire attack, according to Gwenda, lasted no more than ten minutes. While this number is an exaggeration in the minds of investigators, they claimed that the attack likely didn't exceed 30 minutes.

Gwenda finished off the beers and headed to her bedroom to go to sleep. She made no attempt, at that point, to hide the body. She seemingly couldn't care less that her best friend of over 20 years lay dead in her kitchen. The body of Michelle Hoffman-Tamm would rest in a puddle of blood and a pile of rubble for over 24 hours. Gwenda claims that she had no plans for what she should do next. While prosecution would eventually claim that the entire event was pre-mediated, Gwenda stood strong with her story that she had 'blacked-out in a fit of rage' against Michelle.

On the morning of November 9, 2012, Gwenda decided that she had to do something with the body. Even at this point, she had received several calls from Michelle's family asking her if she knew where Michelle was. She knew that she had to get rid of the body.

Gwenda Sloane woke up on November 9 with only the goal of getting rid of Michelle's body. She went to the local hardware store and purchased a box of black plastic outdoor trash bags as well as a large roll of duct tape. She returned to her home to begin her cover-up.

She wrapped Michelle's body in several of the black trash bags. She used almost the entire roll of duct tape wrapping the bags around the body over and over and over again. When she had finished her work, there was absolutely no sight of a body. It simply looked like a trash heap. She had situated the bags in a way that would look wider than a body.

She loaded Michelle's body in to the back of her Subaru and hit the road. She had no intentions of leaving the body anywhere near her own neighborhood. She decided that she would head off to Whakatane, a rural area of the North Island near Rotorua. She figured that this area was secluded enough that no one would find the body.

Shortly after leaving town, she started to look for suitable locations to leave the body. She finally settled on a 1.5 meter deep ditch in Murupara. The ditch was covered with tall grass and vegetation. Also surrounding the area was lots of rubbish and waste. She put the body at the bottom of this deep ditch and buried it in dirt and trash. She quickly entered back into her Subaru and took off. She claims that the entire process of burying the body took less than 5 minutes. She said that no one passed by on the road or would have seen anything happen. For all intents and purposes, she had found a perfect location. Police agreed, stating numerous times that if Gwenda hadn't led police to the body, they likely would never have found it.

Upon returning home, Gwenda rented a carpet cleaning machine at the local store. She claims that she worked all day to clean all of the floors and carpets to free them of blood and evidence. While DNA is impossible to entirely eradicate in such an instance, police never suspected anything when they entered her home. It didn't seem like the typical murder scene.

After setting all of the trash out, there was still one major piece of evidence that had to be taken care of. Michelle had rode her bike over to Gwenda's home. The bike still leaned neatly under Gwenda's car port. She knew that if investigators found the bike at her home, that she would become a prime suspect. Her idea was to get rid of the bike quickly and discreetly. To do this, she took the bike to a store front and put it in a bike stand. While this doesn't seem like a crucial move, it quickly led investigators down many false roads. This was essentially the last element that Gwenda had to get rid of to be free of any evidence. She had accomplished this with no problems.

The most crucial area of the home was the kitchen. This is the entire location that the murder took place. Gwenda claims that she had been in the living room and Michelle was standing in the kitchen when she became enraged. She said that she charged Michelle as she was standing with her back to the living room. She never saw anything coming. She truly never had a chance to defend herself.

Gwenda used some of the trash bags that she had purchased to load up all of the cleaning materials that she used. She had two full trash bags worth of 'evidence' when it was all said and done. Instead of taking them to the dump herself, she simply sat them on the curb for the local trash collection to pick up. Within the next few days, the trash company picked up all of the bags. While this seems extremely minor for the big picture, this is important for the investigation. With all of this being disposed of and the body of Michelle being hidden so well by Gwenda, there was essentially no evidence to break open the case.

The murder was finished. Police knew that the person who had murdered Michelle Hoffman-Tamm was in custody. They also knew that, with the voluntary confession, they would likely be able to avoid a long, drawn out court case. They still had one major aspect of the case to figure out. Why would Gwenda murder her friend and sexual partner of nearly 20 years, seemingly for no reason?

Gwenda Sloane claims that she 'knew that Michelle had taken $20 from her'. Really? Gwenda murdered her best friend due to her belief that she stole $20 from her? This simply didn't add up to investigators.

Gwenda stated that the attack started after the two had been drinking heavily. They were planning to go eat that morning, so she went to the living room to get her wallet. It was at this point that she discovered that she was missing $20 from her wallet. She immediately attacked Michelle and began yelling at her as she punched and stabbed her.

This story would be the last official statement that Gwenda would give as to her motive for killing Michelle. Family member of Michelle, however, have a different suspicion as to why she murdered Michelle.

Many in Michelle's family claim that over the most recent years, Gwenda became increasingly jealous of Inoi. She would come around far less often, instead she would have Michelle come to her home. Many agree that Gwenda wanted more out of their relationship than Michelle wanted to give.

The flip side of the equation is simple. Why would Michelle not want more with Gwenda if they were so close? This leads many to assume that perhaps Michelle had seen a dark side of Gwenda before. Maybe she was scared to go further with her for the fear of her snapping. This is all speculation, of course.

The bottom line is that the murder of Michelle Hoffman-Tamm would famously enter the headlines as the '$20 murder'. The public became wrapped in the story, not able to comprehend how this unfortunate turn of events could all take place as a result of a petty money theft accusation. To this day, many wonder if this was the true motive behind the crime. While the theories are abundant, the fact is that no one truly knows except for Gwenda.

Gwenda officially entered her plea as guilty. This avoided a long, painful court process. She was sentenced to life in prison on February 4, 2013. To the shock of many, she was given the option of a parole hearing after just 17 years. While she would be well into her senior years by that time, it was quite offensive to Michelle's family.

Gwenda was just 43 years old when she murdered Michelle. She was just 44 years old when she was given her life sentence. The most saddening part of this entire case is the impact it has had on Michelle's family. They have been forced to question everyone that they have learned to trust.

"I have lost all trust in the world. I understand when people say that they have lost everything and it's gut-wrenching," Rhys Hoffman, son of Michelle said in a statement at the sentencing hearing. "I never got to make up for all the times I wasn't there for my mum."

The impact of Michelle's family can't be overstated. This trusted woman that was more like family to all of them was the one who ultimately inflicted such pain and suffering. The overall result of this case is one that is justice. While it may not be equal to what happened to Michelle, Gwenda Sloane is behind bars and is in a place where she can't do this to anyone else. No matter what the motive of the murder is, the simple fact that there was a murder is devastating enough to all who were involved and impacted on this case. While this murder may not have grabbed international headlines, its circumstance and result are just as sad and devastating as any other murder that has been in the media.

She Killed Dad

Jessi Dillard

Born on May 28, 1972, Stacey Ann Lannert grew up in what appeared to be a picture-perfect family. She and her sister, Christy, were raised by two loving parents. Tom, their father, worked as a financial consultant, and their mother Deb took on the role of a stay-at-home mom. However, as the two girls got older, their 'ideal' family started to crumble right before their eyes.

"In 1990, life as I knew it ended, for better and for worse," Lannert wrote in her memoir, *Redemption: A Story of Sisterhood, Survival, and Finding Freedom Behind Bars*. "I had committed murder."

Daddy's little girl

In the early 70s, the Lannert family lived in Cedar Rapids, Iowa. Deb was a devoted mother, Lannert recalled in her memoir. As a stay-at-home mom, she kept up with the regular domestic chores, but also spent a lot of time teaching her young daughter. Lannert learned her ABCs by the age of two, and at three, could write her telephone number and her name. Before she turned four years old, she knew how to read.

"We had all of her attention in the early years," Lannert wrote. "I wish we could have frozen time and just stayed in that place forever."

However, Lannert recalls being particularly close to her father – even describing herself as "daddy's little girl." Her father was "like Superman" to her, because he was always prepared to handle any problem she encountered. She remembers him as handsome, with a prominent nose and a strong chin, and a warm, comforting laugh.

"He had beautiful blue eyes that could melt or destroy me – it was his choice," she said. "We stayed up late together even when I was really little. He held me all the time when he finished work or studying."

After dinner, they would share a snack of buttered popcorn from her dad's special yellow Tupperware bowl. He referred to his eldest daughter as "Tiger," and always encouraged her to stand up for herself whenever the kids at school teased her.

"I always felt like everything was right in the world when he was there," she said. "He lavished me with attention, and I could see no wrong in my father. He was just *it* for me."

The family's life was so idyllic, so secure and happy that Lannert said she didn't pay much notice to the "tiny cracks" that were beginning to form in the family's foundation. A car accident that should have killed Tom left him with nothing more than a few scratches, thanks to his blood alcohol level.

"His body was so loose from the alcohol that he slithered right out of the car," Lannert recalled. "He didn't even remember what had happened."

It's not a big deal, she remembers her father telling her. "Everything is going to be fine."

But things weren't fine. The more Tom would drink, the more Deb would nag – and Lannert said the bond she and her father shared became even stronger as his marriage began to fall apart. And when Deb gave away Lannert's beloved dog, Max, she said she started to think her mother was just mean.

"Twenty years later, I found out the truth," she said. "She gave Max away because my dad would come home drunk, trip over my excited dog, and then kick Max. Mom felt awful when she heard the dog yelping in the hallway, and she wanted the dog to be safe. Meanwhile, there I was, almost eight years old, secretly hating her for taking my dog away."

After her eighth birthday, Lannert started to see a different side of the father she'd always admired. He started off by introducing her to a new game called "touch tongues," which progressed rapidly to more forceful activities like genital touching and oral sex.

At first, Lannert said she didn't mind – it didn't hurt her, and it made her father happy. She admitted that she also liked having a secret that made her feel closer to her beloved Daddy. He was "all I needed," she said. But when she was nine years old, her father's molestation got even more aggressive – he started raping her.

"I felt like he was just tearing me apart," she recalls. "It felt like I was literally being ripped in half, and he was saying such hateful things to me. I didn't know what to do."

She also remembers wondering if all fathers did this to their daughters – but said once he actually started raping her, she could tell "that wasn't right," because it was more violent and painful than the "games" they'd been playing prior to that.

"Any man who can hold his daughter down and rape her is evil," she said. "And nobody stopped him. No one."

Lannert's father told her there was no use tattling to her mom – according to Tom, Deb already knew about what he was doing to their daughter. For Lannert, it felt like a betrayal, and she began to blame her mother for the abuse that her father was forcing on her.

The bitterness Lannert felt toward her mother only intensified when her parents divorced when she was 12 years old.

"I became resentful even more so of my mother for leaving my dad, and almost even took his side in the whole divorce," she said.

She made the decision to continue living with her father when her mother moved out – even though he was still abusing her regularly, anywhere from three to five times each week. To Lannert, the abuse wasn't coming from the same man who she'd been so close to, growing up.

"At some point, I separated my dad into two different people," she said. "My dad, and then Tom, the man who would abuse me."

A deadly misunderstanding

A babysitter finally caught on to Lannert's discomfort, and asked the young girl if her father had been hurting her. When Lannert replied that he was, the babysitter tried to tell Lannert's mother – but Deb didn't think much of it. In fact, years later, she admitted that at the time, she'd thought the babysitter simply meant Lannert had been spanked by her father.

"What I felt was that he loved them and he would not hurt them. I thought he loved his daughters," Deb told ABC News. "I feel like I failed to protect my children ... and I will never ever forget that. I will never live this down no matter what."

In Lannert's memoir, she describes how her maternal grandfather had "fondled" her mother, Deb – and, according to Lannert's account, the sexual abuse going on at her mother's childhood home also "was never acknowledged."

"But because allegations weren't made – the words 'I am being molested' were never spoken – the situation could be quietly ignored," Lannert wrote.

This kind of misunderstanding is part of the reason why Lannert now advocates for victims of sexual abuse – and speaks out about the value of teaching kids what is acceptable and what isn't.

"That's why it's so important to find the real words," she explained. "If we don't name it, people can make it mean what they want it to mean. If you say, 'my father raped me,' they get it. But I didn't even have that word."

Eventually, Lannert couldn't stand it anymore, and made the decision to live with her mother. But her younger sister Christy continued to live with Tom, which made Lannert feel uneasy. Christy had only ever suffered physical abuse at the hands of their father, Lannert said.

"I felt like I was protecting her by taking the sexual abuse," she explained. "If he'd hit her, I'd just thank God that's all it was."

When Christy was in first grade, the beatings began. After her father was killed, she told ABC News that by the time she was 12 years old, Tom was pushing to drink alcohol with him. And, she said, the more he drank, the more violent and abusive his behaviour would become. Even decades later, she can't handle revisiting the house where she grew up with her older sister.

"I don't care to see the stairs that he used to kick me down," she said. "I don't, I don't want to see the windows that I would have to climb out at night, so I didn't have to wake up being choked."

One day, after Christy called her older sister begging for help, Lannert decided to go back to the house.

"I walked in and opened the door, and there he was," she said, remembering how Tom immediately threw her down and began raping her. "When he got done raping me, he kicked me – and I got smart probably for the first time ever. I was going to fight."

That day, she said, was the last straw. One month later, the two girls snuck into their father's house. Lannert had argued with Tom earlier that day, and the sisters were coming home late at night – hoping their father would already be passed out. They often sneaked in through the window in the basement, Lannert explained.

He was passed out on the couch, but Christy accidentally woke him. He started yelling at her, while Lannert retreated to the basement to grab Tom's gun. By the time she made it back up the stairs, she said, he'd passed out again. Almost without thinking, she shot him in the collarbone – and he sat up immediately.

"All of a sudden, he just started yelling," she said. "I remember thinking, 'he can't get up, because if he gets up, he'll kill us.' So I picked the gun back up and just closed my eyes and pulled the trigger."

Lannert also remembers thinking that Tom "didn't deserve to live," and Christy felt the same way. She told police at the time that she "may have" told her sister to "just do it."

The next day, the girls talked to an adult friend about what they'd done, and the friend helped her get rid of the gun. When she called the police, she told them she'd come home to find her father dead on the sofa – likely killed during a burglary.

Eventually, though, Lannert confessed. She told authorities that she'd killed her father because she "hated him" and that "he needed to die." Christy agreed.

"I had this mind-set, 'this is going to end,'" she explained. "I wanted him to stop. I wanted him to know we're leaving and I can stand up to (him). I didn't ever really make a conscious choice. I guess somewhere in my mind I did, but I wanted him to know that I could fight against him."

She claimed the killing was in self-defense, but prosecutors argued that she hadn't suffered any abuse. In fact, even when police asked Lannert if her father had been abusing her and she told them that he had, no rape-kit test was ever administered. They didn't even ask for more details.

Determining the motive

One officer, though, had her back. Lt. Tom Schulte listened to Lannert's story after she made her confession. She explained to him that the many years of abuse had worn her down, and driven her to commit the crime.

"The last thing I told that young lady when I left her – and it was late that night, I told her, 'I'll be there for you,'" he said.

However, Schulte's testimony didn't support the argument the prosecution was making against Lannert.

The motive for the murder, prosecutors alleged, was money. They accused Lannert of forging his checks and using his credit cards – and said that with Tom out of the picture, Lannert stood to inherit almost $100,000 from her father's estate.

"I had his permission to use the account," Lannert said. "I wasn't working at the time, and he didn't want me working. It was a way of him isolating me."

Many people also questioned Lannert's choice to continue living with her father when her parents' marriage ended, if he was truly an abusive man. But she said that at the time, it was the only option that "made sense" for her.

"We got sent back and forth between the two of them a lot, and there were times that he didn't hurt me," she explained. "My father loved me, not the abuser who would rape me. They weren't (the same person) in my mind."

To Lannert, judging the decision she made as a child who was suffering through tremendous abuse does nothing to help the situation – and can make life even more difficult for the victims of these kinds of crimes.

"A lot of times, we wind up seeing more victimization because of the choices we make," she said. "My life was hell, and I was struggling just to be able to survive every day – and then, after the fact, I have to face answers of why I didn't do this or that. It's harsh."

Lannert also asserts that she did try to leave, moving 7,000 miles away to live with her mother on the island of Guam. But when she received a desperate call from Christy, she couldn't ignore the fact that her sister might need her help.

"All I really cared about was making sure that Christy never had to go through that pain that I had to go through, ever," she said. "I never wanted that for her."

She'd even tried to convince her father to let Christy leave with her, but Tom refused. According to Lannert, all he wanted Christy for was to maintain what little control he still had over his eldest daughter.

Lannert's lawyer tried to argue the defense of insanity or mental defect, attempting to use the "battered spouse syndrome" to explain her behaviour – however, in a pre-trial ruling, the court ordered limited mention of the term.

Still, several expert witnesses were brought in to testify at the trial and conceded that Lannert exhibited signs of abuse. The jury also heard from both Lannert and the babysitter she'd tried to confide in about the ongoing abuse – and, in some states, if a jury believed the allegations of abuse, Lannert's plea of self-defense could have been accepted even though her father had been passed out drunk when she shot him.

But in Missouri, the plea wasn't considered to be valid, since Lannert wasn't in immediate danger when she made the decision to pull the trigger and end her father's life. The prosecution was able to convince the jury, which found Lannert guilty of murder in the first degree. After just a one-week trial, the verdict was read – and, in Missouri, a conviction of murder in the first degree carried a mandatory sentence of life in prison, without the possibility of parole.

"The verdict was absolutely appropriate," said McCulloch. "It's the verdict that should have been returned. She got the sentence that she deserved, and that's where she ought to be."

For her part in the murder, Christy pled guilty to the charge of conspiracy to commit murder and spent two and a half years behind bars.

Despite having spent many years investigating sex crimes, and being the first officer to question Lannert after her father's murder, Schulte was never called to testify. Lannert admitted that she felt abandoned and betrayed for many years, until she learned that he would have testified on her behalf, had he been given the opportunity.

Once Lannert was in prison, Schulte said he made the decision not to contact her and explain what had happened. Any contact between them, he believed, would risk calling into question his affidavit – which noted all his observations from the night he had interviewed her.

Several members of the jury also came forward after Lannert had been sentenced, outraged that they hadn't been presented with all of the facts regarding the sexual and physical abuse Lannert had suffered at the hands of her father. A statement was issued by the United States Court of Appeals for the Eight Circuit after Lannert filed a petition for appeal, claiming that the Missouri self-defense statute indicates no specific time frame in which an act of self-defense can occur, following an initial act of aggression or provocation.

"It is therefore deeply troubling that the jury was not completely informed of the scope of the abuse Lannert suffered, her fear, or her rage that her sister may also have been victimized by their father," the statement read. "This evidence of battered spouse syndrome might have placed Lannert's actions in proper context, and may have allowed a jury to conclude that Lannert was not the initial aggressor on the night of her father's death, potentially resulting in a very different outcome than what she faces today."

Still, the court refused to accept Lannert's argument that "a man who raped his daughter, when she was in the third grade, made him 'the initial aggressor,' and the author of his own doom." It also determined that battered spouse syndrome cannot be considered a defense in itself, but rather indicates support for a claim of self-defense.

Released by the grace of God

After exhausting her appeals, Lannert petitioned the court for clemency for years. The affidavit from Schulte was a key part of the request. Her lawyers finally launched a publicity campaign on her behalf, which allowed Lannert to share her story to influential figures like Montel Williams, Nancy Grace, and Oprah Winfrey.

"Having to go public was the worst moment for me," Lannert recalled. "It was so shameful. How was I going to be able to look anybody in the eye again? But then I did it, and I started receiving letters from so many people, saying 'you could have been me.'"

Lannert had spent 18 years in prison before Missouri Governor Matt Blunt looked at her file. In January of 2009, Blunt commuted Lannert's life sentence to twenty years after undertaking an "extensive review of the evidence" – finally, after almost two decades of incarceration, Lannert was free.

"(I was released) by the grace of God and the perseverance of two wonderful attorneys, a police detective who never gave up, and a governor who had a lot of courage," she said.

However, St. Louis County prosecutor Bob McCulloch, who persuaded the court that Lannert was a manipulative liar who killed her father solely for financial reasons, maintained that she deserved to spend the rest of her life behind bars.

"I have not changed my mind at all about Stacey Lannert. She murdered her father for his inheritance, and solely for his inheritance," he told ABC News in March of 2009. "She was never sexually abused by her father or anyone else, and she ought to be back in the penitentiary, and shame on Governor Blunt for letting her out."

According to McCulloch, Tom Lannert was a "bad father" and a "bad drunk" – not a rapist. He claimed Lannert was "lying through her teeth," and that there was no evidence to support her allegations that she had been sexually abused.

"The only credible evidence of any sort of motive is that she did it for the money," he said. "And she's not going to get her hands on it unless she – unless she takes out her father."

To this day, Lannert denies McCulloch's allegations that she "spent wildly" and was only interested in the $500,000 estate that she stood to inherit in the case of her father's death.

"I wanted him to leave me alone; I wanted him to leave her alone," she said. "I didn't really necessarily want him to die, but I didn't want him to be able to... hurt us again, to be able to get us."

Throughout her time in prison, Lannert said it was her own dedication to her faith that kept her patient – even during harder times. Although she worked hard at maintaining a positive attitude, she admitted it was difficult.

"There were times I gave up," she recalled. "I really believed I would spend the rest of my life in prison."

While Lannert agrees that since she did "break one of society's rules," her time in prison was well-deserved – but she said she felt she had no other way of escaping her father's incessant abuse.

"There was nowhere to run to – I didn't feel like there was anywhere I could go that he couldn't find me," she said. "He would tell us how he would find us: the car was registered in his name, he could track me through the social security card number, and he would tell me how he would find me and I believed him."

Since her release from prison, Lannert has founded Healing Sisters, a non-profit organization and resource website dedicated to help women who have suffered abuse. She hopes her work will someday help to end sexual abuse in America.

"Secrets lose their power when they're shared," she explained. "I think that every woman who's been abused thinks at one point in time, 'I'm going to kill you.' There's power in the thought – but not in the actual act itself, and I don't think people understand that. Now, not only do I have the shame and guilt of what he did to me, I also have the shame and guilt of my actions."

She also now recognizes that a more powerful action would have been to turn her father in – to put him "in the defendant's seat," she said, "and make my accusations against him."

"I was free in my heart."

Still, during her time in prison, Lannert was able to do some healing – and was finally able to deal with what her father put her through for all those years. While she said she's certainly pleased to be out, prison made her confront many of the uncomfortable feelings she had been pushing down.

"I couldn't run away from my past at all," she said. "The compassion and encouragement and support that I have been met with from other women who went through the same thing just really made me feel like I wasn't alone."

She also kept herself busy in prison by investing her time in a positive hobby – learning to train dogs to help people with disabilities. When she was finally released, she met up with Schulte in St. Louis – and he asked her to train his dog.

"I feel a connection with him that I'll probably never feel with another human being, because he was the first person who helped me, who believed me," she said. "It took a long time for it to come to fruition, but he did stand behind me and helped. And I'm just very thankful."

With some closure on the situation, Lannert said she can now see that Tom, her abuser, and the father she loved were the same person all along.

"I had to, in order to forgive myself for the action that I took, because there were moments that I missed my father," she admitted. "I had to forgive him in order to be able to forgive myself – but there's a difference between forgiving and forgetting."

Forgiving, she said, gave her the ability to move past what she has endured, and finally look toward the future.

"If I don't forgive him, then I'm in prison – it might not be a physical prison, but it's psychological prison," she said. "You know, I was incarcerated, and I was free in my heart. The rest was geography."

Although she felt free in her heart, it's nothing compared to the true freedom of being released from prison. Adjusting to life outside of jail has been challenging, as Lannert said she's not used to being able to do whatever she wants, whenever she wants.

"I ask for permission all the time," she said. "I need to learn how to break that. It doesn't seem real to me yet. But I'm working on it, and I'm so happy. I can't believe I got this second chance at life, so I'm just excited."

While Lannert knows some people still won't believe her story, or might judge her for how she dealt with her father's abuse, she said she chooses not to hold it against them.

"Every person in America is entitled to their own opinion," she stated. "I can't judge them."

HUSBAND KILLER : THE TRUE STORY OF TRACEY GRISSOM

28

SARAH CAMDEN

Claiming to be a victim of rape and other abuses, a distraught Tracey Grissom would travel to her ex-husband Hunter's workplace and shoot him six times in the back, receiving a twenty-five-year life sentence for his murder.

Her defense attorney would argue that Tracey was motivated by post-traumatic stress disorder caused by her Hunter's constant abuse and sexual assaults. One jury member had even asked the judge to be lenient in her sentencing as they were not allowed to hear details of her Hunter's alleged abuses (beatings, rape, sodomy).

But what really happened in the years that led up to May 15th, 2012? Was she in fact the victim of years of abuse by a psychotic husband? Or did she want to cash in on his $100,000 life insurance policy?

INSTANT ATTRACTION

The couple would meet during a dinner party in 2003 in Tuscaloosa, Alabama. Tracey was twenty-one years old and going through a divorce. She had a son, James Michael, from the previous marriage.

Family and friends would describe the union as "love at first sight." Hunter was blown away by the young Tracey's blue eyes and facial beauty.

"For him, it was love at first sight," crime author William Phelps said. "She was gorgeous."

A whirlwind courtship would ensue and the couple would elope in 2004.

"In the beginning, it was good," Tracey told CBS' 48 hours. "We had a friendship. Just your normal, honeymoon phase marriage."

"He was fun," Tracey said. "And he was attractive."

Hunter was two years younger than Tracey, however, and his mother felt that he had jumped the gun too early in the relationship.

Her words proved to be prophetic as after only eight months into the marriage, the marriage went south.

According to Tracey, their marital problems began with Hunter's drug addiction.

"I had caught him smoking marijuana," Tracey said. "Doing illegal things could cause a problem and I couldn't risk losing my son over."

Tracey claimed that she threatened her new spouse with a divorce but Hunter gave her his word that he would stop with his drug use. She stated that the relationship improved and the decided to start a construction company together.

"I took out an equity line to start a company," Tracey said. "Which was Grissom Construction. It was all in my name."

Hunter specialized in building elaborate boat docks. He had an artistic eye and could do docks, stairs, and other accouterments. The business began to grow in short order.

"They're going to take on the world," Phelps said. "They're going to be entrepreneurs and they're gonna make it."

They then had a daughter of their own, Anna Grace. The child was a long time coming for the couple. They had been trying for a long time as Tracey had five miscarriages before Anna Grace was born.

"She was premature," Tracey recalled. "Her heart and lungs were not developed. A very stressful time."

Behind closed doors things were rocky. On the surface, however, things looked good. They had a young family and were making money.

"All-American family," Phelps said. "White-picket fence. The whole nine yards. Middle-class. Suburbia. Maybe the Prince Charming that she's been waiting for."

But again, this was only on the surface. Tracey harbored secrets of her own. One of which was her own addiction to prescription drugs.

"Psychologically, there's something going on here," Phelps said. "There's something going on behind those beautiful eyes and it ain't good."

Tracey would often turn on on the children, showing off her temper. Then she would turn on Hunter.

"This would cause friction in the marriage," Phelps said. "And where there's friction, there's fire."

SETTING THE STAGE

Tracey would later state that Hunter would "act strangely" shortly before she filed divorce. She was a registered nurse and gave him an over-the-counter drug test. According to her, Hunter tested posted for marijuana, Oxycontin, opiates, and methamphetamine.

Hunter would later be arrested for marijuana possession but his family would insist that he never did the harder drugs.

Tracey would file for divorce in the summer of 2010 after six years of marriage. According to her, this would prompt physical abuse from Hunter.

Hunter had to move out but their divorce agreement would allow him access to the home.

"In September of 2010," Tracey recalled. "That was the first time he physically hit me. It (the abuse) got progressively worse. He had made the comments that if I told anybody he would kill me. I believed him."

Hunter' co-workers and family members would have a different take on the situation, however. His co-workers remembered a time when she tracked him down at one of the jobs and made a scene.

"She's screaming, jumping on him," Hunter's co-worker said. "Said something about him having another girlfriend and used the expression about, 'You are mine. I'll kill you. I'll kill you. You are mine."

"She's borderline demonic," Hunter's mother said. " mean, I absolutely believe—that she is that troubled."

Hunter's family continued to believe that he did not abuse Tracey.

"He did not have an abusive, an angry bone in his body," Hunter's aunt Gina said. "In fact, we kind of laughed at him because he was too laid-back."

The divorce was finalized in October of 2010.

EVIDENCE OF ABUSE?

Loran Richards was the first of Tracey's friends to notice the minor injuries on her body. She would inquire about the bruises but the answers she received were always evasive. Seeing Tracey with a black eye, however, forced her to try and get more answers.

"I said, Tracey, you may have terrible luck," Richards recalled. "But nobody is so unlucky that they trip, fall down the stairs, and hit their face on a baseball in the eye socket. So don't give me a lame excuse. You don't have to give me any excuse, but let's take a picture."

Tracey broke down. She gave her friend all of the grisly details, detailing the abuse she suffered at the hands of Hunter. Loran then became her advocate, taking pictures of Tracey's injuries. She would later state that she saw blood stains and other signs of abuse at Tracey's home.

THAT FATEFUL NIGHT

Now divorced, Hunter would arrive at Tracey's home on November 22nd, 2010.

According to Tracey, he then became enraged when Tracey told him that she had spent the night with a new lover.

"He told me that he was gonna kill me," Tracey recalled. Tracey stated that she tried to escape, running into the closet in order to "get away from the kids and to pray." Tracey's eleven-year-old son from a previous relationship was in the home as was the four-year-old daughter they have together.

Hunter caught up with her and knocked her to the ground. He tied a belt around her ankles and then began choking her.

Half-conscious, Tracey alleged to have been raped and sodomized.

The brutal attack would leave Tracey unconscious. She would wake up the next morning on the bathroom floor.

"I called Hunter," Tracey recalled. "I told him that I was bleeding and that I was hurt and that I needed help. And he told me, 'Fuck you. I hope you die."

Tracey wound up in the emergency room after the attack. Hospital records would show that she had a laceration on her head, bruises, and ligature marks on her feet.

Tracey would then be referred to the Turning Point domestic violence center.

Marian Waters would describe Tracey's injuries as among the worst she had ever seen in a twenty-year career.

Waters would testify that Tracey had suffered a horrific assault. She described her mental state as typical of someone who had just been raped; fearful, jumpy, fearing for her life.

Tracey had suffered a hematoma on her side that was the side of a grapefruit. She also claimed to have experienced rectal nerve damage which would require surgery as well as torn vaginal muscles requiring her to have a hysterectomy.

Police were called and Hunter would be arrested for rape, sodomy, kidnapping and domestic violence.

"And at that point, I feared for my life," Tracey recalled. "And I feared for my children's life."

A HIDDEN AGENDA

Hunter would be freed on bail but Tracey got a restraining order against him. She bought a gun and did not go anywhere unarmed.

She took photos of her injuries on the night of the alleged attack and texted them to Loran. Later, they would take more pictures.

Angered, Hunter would stop paying her spousal and child support. Tracey, however, may have had another scenario in mind for obtaining money.

She had forced Hunter to take out a $103,000 life insurance policy around the time their daughter was born.

On May 24, 2012, the day before Tracey shot Hunter, she would place a call to MetLife that was recorded.

"Thank you for calling MetLife, this is Pam. May I please have your name?"

"Tracey Grissom."

Tracey would then explain that she was angry that her husband stopped making payments on his policy. During their divorce proceedings, he had agreed to continue paying the premiums. Tracey stated she was calling to make sure that they had the correct address on file.

"Is there anything else I can do for you today?

"That's gonna be it!" Tracey said, hanging up.

"Well, May 14th was just like any other day," Tracey said, explaining the call to the insurance company. "However, I had moved four different times. Me and my children were running. We were running from Hunter. So I had called the company to let them know that they had my old address and to make an address change."

FALSE RAPE?

Shelly Standridge was hired by Hunter to defend him in the rape case. She would state that Hunter denied raping or even assaulting Tracey that night. Hunter did, however, admit to the fact that he and his wife had consensual sex that night...Rough consensual sex.

"So that night," Standridge said. "Hunter said that she was depressed and claiming she was going to kill herself. She was saying she wanted their relationship to work."

So she undressed in front of him. Her beauty was always impossible for Hunter to resist.

The two had sex despite Hunter having a new girlfriend at home.

Hunter's aunt, Gina, believed that Tracey wanted to kill Hunter before the rape case went to court.

"He had a new girlfriend, he was living with her," Phelps said. "He was moving on with his life. Hunter would claim that Tracey was jealous, obsessive, even stalked them."

"Hunter had moved on," Hunter's aunt said. "There was some court dates coming up that would prove that Hunter was innocent. There were court dates coming up that he would get visitation to his daughter. She had a lot to lose."

Tracey was on the anti-anxiety drug Klonopin. Hunter would tell his attorney that Tracey would take more than her prescribed dose. Because of this, she fell and cut her head. Hunter would then leave the house around 10:30 pm and go to his father's house. Tracey would call him hours later, at 3:20 am.

Hunter would state that Tracey had called to threaten him. She told him if he didn't want the responsibility of the children then she would make it where he would never be able to see them again.

Hunter's attorney did not know what Tracey's motive was for crying rape. She was very upset that he had a girlfriend.

MORE LIES...

Hunter would be arrested nearly twelve hours later, to his total shock.

Tracey would give her side of the story to the police which later is proven to be false.

She would tell police that Hunter had thrown her against the bathtub around 10 pm and claim to be unconscious until 4 am the next morning.

"But her phone records show she was on the phone all night, so she was never unconscious," Standridge said. "She was also using her data at 10:42 that night. She was using it again at 10:50 that night. ... She sends a text to her boyfriend at 1:49 am. She sends a text to her friend at 2:07 am. She sends another text to her boyfriend at 2:07 am."

Tracey would blame the calls on Hunter.

"All I do know is I was not the only person using my phone that night," Tracey said, suggesting that Hunter used her phone.

Medical records would show that Tracey's head wound was "purely superficial".

Only one suture was needed.

Furthermore, there was nothing on the medical record to support the fact that Tracey experienced vaginal and rectal tears. She did have bruises on her ankle and legs but the photos taken by police at the emergency room would not resemble the same photos that Tracey and her friend Loran would take days later. In the photos taken at the emergency room, an area of Tracey's body has no bruises. Days later, there is discoloration.

Tracey's attorney would blame the discrepancy on "blood thinners" which would cause Tracey to bruise easily.

There was also a discrepancy in her phone records. She would take a photo of her inner thigh, a deep bruise. This area of her body was not photographed by police during her emergency room visit. But on December 9th, almost two weeks later, Tracey took a photo of her inner thigh with the deep bruise

"He (Hunter) told me that he would make it to where nobody would ever want me," Tracey said after a 2010 attack. "I didn't report it because I thought he would kill me."

THE FINAL STRAW

Tracey woke up pissed on May 15th, 2012.

Hunter had been ordered to pay $2,100 a month for the rest of his life. He was not complying with the court order claiming that he was "out of work."

Tracey stated that she was on her way to a job interview when she saw a Grissom Construction sign out of the corner of her eye.

She stated that her initial plan was to take a photograph of Hunter at the job site in order to show proof that he was working as part of her litigation.

"I was getting ready to take the picture and when I looked up he was standing almost directly towards the front of the boat trailer," Tracey said. "He was looking back directly at me. He had this face, that's like mean - just, I don't know how to describe it. I mean, I see it over and over like it's right there all the time. He flipped me the bird, which to me was kinda like, 'Yeah I'm workin. Screw you.' And at that point, I panicked. At that point, I didn't know what else to do except to defend myself."

Tracey started firing. The first shot hit Hunter in the arm. He started to run and she fired again repeatedly. One of the bullets punctured Hunter's heart and he died of massive internal bleeding.

William Dockery was working with Hunter and was an eyewitness to the shooting. Hunter had turned to Dockery before the shooting and told him to "call the law". Before Dockery could pick up his cell phone, Tracey had commenced shooting.

Tracey then pulled out her own cell phone and called the cops on herself. She tearfully described that she had just murdered her husband.

CONFESSION

Tracey told detectives exactly what was going through her mind when she came upon Hunter at the construction site.

"Tell me about what happened," the detective said. "What led up to...what's going on."

"In November of 2010, he beat me unconscious and raped me...and, and left me for dead....and, and I finally pressed charges against him and he told me that he would make my life a living hell...and that's what he's done."

"What, what happened this morning that led up to you going..."

"I was going to work and I saw him...and he's been claiming that he-he's not working. And, so I pulled in there to take a picture of him...cause it was the truck that's still in my name...and the boat that's still in my name...and the trailer that's still in my name...He just stared at me and flipped me off...and I just went in there and shot him...I just shot him, I shot him, and I shot him."

Tracey would be distraught and tearful during her interrogation room confession. A few weeks later, however, she would call the insurance company to let them know that Hunter had died.

"Well, I was actually calling because I didn't know what I needed to do ... Hunter passed away May 15th and I actually am going a court case right now because it was due to self-defense..."

Hunter's family went ballistic over this. Tracey would claim that she had no money but she continued to pay his life insurance premiums.

"Even through the times when she's screamin' that she's destitute and has no money ... she continued to pay life insurance premium," Hunter's mother said.

"I don't think my sister concocted a story," Tracey's sister said. "Just so she could get insurance money. ... But that's all they (the prosecution) had."

THE TRIAL

Tracey's allegations of rape and sodomy would not be allowed in court testimony. She was allowed, however, to detail the effects of Hunter's abuse on her were.

Taking the stand, Tracey would lift up her shirt in court and show herself wearing a colostomy bag. She stated that she had undergone several surgeries after her husband's daily rapes wherein she suffered permanent rectal and vaginal damage.

Hunter's family was then allowed to speak at the hearing.

"This tremendous loss has changed me," Hunter's mother, Melanie Garner said. "And I don't know how to change back."

Chloe, Hunter's sister, had a victim's services officer read her letter in court.

"Tracey is psychotic," Chloe wrote. "She is the most selfish person human being on this earth."

"Every mother should pray every night that your son doesn't fall in love with someone like Tracey," Hunter's aunt, Gina Grissom said. "There have been lots of allegations against Hunter. We've never believed anything that has come out of her (Tracey's) mouth."

His aunt then looked directly at Tracey.

"Hunter was proud of his name. Why would you still choose to use our name, and bring it down?" suggesting that if Tracey hated him so much why didn't she go revert to her maiden name after the divorce.

The jurors would find Tracey guilty of murder. She would be sentenced to twenty-five years in prison.

One of the jurors, Janice Kelly, would contact Grissom's attorney Warren Freeman the morning after the trial. She had remorse over her decision and said that she wouldn't have convicted her had they had the rapes and abuse allegations been introduced as evidence.

"I feel I made a mistake," Kelly said. "If I had to do it over again, we'd have had a hung jury. We didn't get her side. She did not get a fair trial."

"We voted to convict because there was no dispute that Tracey shot Hunter," the jury foreman wrote in a letter that was addressed in the courthouse. "Jurors didn't believe prosecutor claims that she did it in order to collect a life insurance policy. We felt the shooting was a crime of passion, not for financial gain and that she should be sentenced accordingly. I wish we had seen evidence of the rape allegation. We feel that she just 'lost it.'"

"It's not fair, it's not fair!" Tracey sobbed as she was led out of the courthouse and to jail.

"We think the sentencing was too harsh," Tracey's attorney Warren Freeman said. "Considering you have the foreperson of the jury actually saying, we don't feel like she should be punished according to being found guilty of murder. Let's just say that there will be a basis for a new trial, and part of it will be something that the jurors saw that they weren't supposed to see and I'm going to just leave it at that until I file my motion."

"My son died running for his life," Hunter's mother said. "I don't know what was running through his mind but I hear him say 'momma.'"

"People who think that I murdered him in cold blood," Tracey said. "Either don't know the whole story or don't know everything that's happened.

Tracey was asked on CBS' 48 hours if she regretted pulling the trigger on that fateful day.

"No," she said flatly. "Because if I hadn't I would be dead. I truly believe that."

"She has a way of making everything she does look right," Hunter's aunt, Gina scoffed.

AMBER CUMMINGS

On the surface, James and Amber Cummings had it all.

They had been married for twelve years. James had inherited millions of dollars from his father and they owned a home in the peaceful, seaside town of Belfast, Maine.

"On paper, they were a couple that looked as if they had everything," forensic psychologist Paula Orange said. "Definitely one of those cases where looks are more than deceiving. They are downright deadly."

The couple met in Fort Bragg, California. Amber was a tall brunette while James was overweight and had an awkward vibe about him.

Amber found him charming, however, and would later describe him as the "nicest guy she'd ever met." She would marry him at 19 years of age and things looked bright for the young couple until Amber got pregnant.

"That is when his personality started to change," Orange said. "He would drive away Amber's family members in California and seek to keep her isolated. This brought much consternation to Amber's side of the family, obviously. There was one heart-breaking instance where Amber's mother and sister went to a neighbor's yard just to get a glimpse of Amber's daughter riding her tricycle."

James wanted no outside influence on Amber or their daughter so he began moving the family around. They left California when Amber turned five and moved to Texas. Then they traveled the country in a motor home until 2007 when the finally settled in Belfast, Maine.

"My husband said that he hated people and that he didn't care where we moved," Amber said. "I always wanted to live in a nice, small town in Maine."

EARLY LIFE

James' life seemed to have been one of trouble even though he was born into wealth.

His father would be murdered by one of his former employees in 1997 which was preceded by James making headline news as he videotaped his own mother doing heroin.

James would have numerous run-ins with the law himself.

"He had a bunch of assault charges," Orange said. "Some were cases where he was the victim. Others were cases where he was the perpetrator. When he was the perp, his father's money always bailed him out."

According to some Internet rumors, James' father had allegedly injured himself while getting off a forklift on one of the docks in the Fort Bragg harbor, breaking his knee in the fall.

Cummings then went to a friend's house and fell to the ground outside claiming that he "tripped in a hole." James' father then sued the owners of the property and won.

"That gives you an idea of the kind of guy James' father was," Orange said. "Rumors abound on the internet and in the Fort Bragg community about how he acquired his wealth. None of it is verifiable aside from the fact that the majority of the trust is funneled through a trailer park, which is odd."

Cummings Sr. would own many businesses and it would be one of his employees, a man named Williams Vargas who would gun him down.

Vargas detonated a homemade bomb he called a "firecracker" outside Cummings' home. The disgruntled employee then panicked as one of Cummings' neighbors drove by and blocked his escape. Cummings Sr. then came out with his own gun to investigate the blast which shattered his window.

Vargas then pulled out his own gun and shot Cummings. He had been working for Cummings at the Noyo Harbor trailer park and was allowed to live there in exchange for labor. But he began having problems with other residents which he would blame Cummings Sr. for.

Cummings, 77 years old at the time of his murder, had built his wealth by running restaurants, motels, a fish-processing plant as well as trailer parks. He also owned the Depot Mall shopping center and a McDonald's restaurant.

``Jim was quite an entrepreneur. He had quite a lot of land holdings, in some key areas, really, in the harbor and other areas around," former City Manager Gary Milliman said.

James Jr. would be the beneficiary of his father's death. He would tell people that he made his living "selling off Texas real estate" but the truth was that he was a trust fund kid living off the businesses that his father created.

The trust fund started off by giving Jams a whopping ten million dollars a year. The funds would deplete rapidly, however, as James would have a six-year legal battle against trustees whom he thought were mismanaging the money.

His mental illness would grow worse as his finances decreased.

NEO-NAZI SYMPATHIES

"He would go on daily rants about Barack Obama," Orange said. "Which would seem harmless at first until Amber realized that James was, in fact, a white supremacist. He began spending his days hunting down rare Nazi artifacts on the Internet and purchasing them."

James had applied to the National Socialist Movement, one of the largest neo-Nazi clubs in the country. He had written numerous white supremacy organizations on-line and began to mix toxic chemicals in their kitchen sink while telling Amber about his desire to make a "dirty bomb."

James had hired a pair of contractors to paint the interior of the house. The painters would later testify to witnessing James berate his wife. He would tell the men about his guns and go on about Adolf Hitler.

Thinking he had an eager audience, James bragged about his collection of silverware and plate settings that he claimed to have been used by Hitler himself.

"Check this out," James showed a swastika flag to the painter. "This was real. Not a knock-off. They actually waved this same flag while Hitler spoke."

James would run his household as if he were Hitler himself, marching around the home wearing a black hat and uniform with a Nazi armband.

Working himself up into a Nazi-like frenzy of rage, he would then abuse Amber physically, emotionally and sexually.

"He stripped away whatever self-esteem she had," Orange said. "He had no friends himself and didn't allow her to have any either."

As the years went by, James developed paranoid schizophrenic tendencies which had given birth to ideas that grew more bizarre with time. The married couple slept in separate bedrooms and James had guns placed under both of their pillows "just in case."

On one occasion, Amber left the home for an extended period of time. James immediately became enraged upon her arrival back. He demanded to know where she was and who she was with. Amber had gone to meet with a home-schooling group which they both previously agreed would be a good idea.

James went ballistic, berating Amber and throwing his sharpened Nazi knives against the wall.

CHILD ABUSE

James did not limit his abuse to Amber. His paranoid anger soon extended to their daughter, Clara.

This became evident to Amber when their daughter had come across James' collection of Nazi knives and began examining them.

"Leave those alone!" James screamed as he ran into the room and grabbed the box of knives away from the girl. "These belonged to the Führer! The Führer!"

Amber had very little self-esteem left, but she intervened when James would physically abuse their daughter. She would throw herself between the two and take the beating herself.

This would only incite James further as the would beat Amber then march up to Clara's room and continue his abuse.

"He kept them isolated and feeling helpless," Orange said. "They tried to escape on a few occasions but he caught them, keeping them locked in the house. She thought he had some kind of superhuman power."

CHILD PORNOGRAPHY

Seeking new outlets, James' mind became so perverted that he soon began indulging in child pornography. He showed his collection to Amber who shuddered in horror.

"Which one do you like best?" he would ask his wife, pointing to a series of pictures on the scream.

In addition to the child pornography, James began teaching his daughter to see the world through his racist viewpoint.

"This is equal-opportunity hatred," he preached to his daughter. "We can hate everybody."

"He was deluded," Orange said. "He actually saw himself as the second coming of Hitler. He began seeing his daughter as his future helper, someone who would be in charge of 'reconditioning' women and children after he declared war on the United States."

James wanted to build a torture chamber in the basement of the house. He told Amber about his desire to kill people and "peel the skin off their bones." He also obsessed on the Showtime television series, "Dexter", which featured a serial killer as the protagonist. James would then take long walks around the Belfast area, daydreaming about living out his 'Dexter' fantasy.

"He constantly talked about the different ways of killing and torturing people and hiding their bodies," Amber said. "He used to say it was a need in him."

THE FINAL STRAW

"The abuse happened incrementally for her," Orange said. "It is easy to sit back and judge a person like her, saying that she should have just left. But she was like a frog in a pot of cool water before it starts to boil. The abuse started small at first then bit by bit it increased as her self-esteem diminished. But when it came to protecting her daughter, she had to act."

One December 9th, 2008, Amber Cummings finally had enough.

She got up like she normally did after another night of abuse by her husband.

"Amber discovered James messing around with the chemicals in the kitchen," Orange said. "He said that he would bury her in the backyard if he said anything."

She sent her daughter downstairs to eat breakfast while she pulled out a .45 caliber pistol from underneath her pillow.

Then she held the gun underneath her own throat.

"Amber's first thought was to kill herself," Orange said. "But then she saw her daughter's doll in the room. She shuddered to think of her daughter spending the rest of her childhood with her father as she realized that it was only a matter of time before James' obsession with child pornography would make him do something to Clara. So she had to seek an alternative course of action."

Amber would later tell court-appointed psychologists that James' infatuation with child pornography and his "sexual attraction to young girls" made her believe that he was becoming obsessed with their daughter.

Fueled by her protective maternal instinct, Amber entered the bedroom where James was sleeping. She never had any gumption to stand up for herself when James abused her.

But when it came to protecting her daughter, a whole new Amber showed up.

She pointed the gun at the back of James' head and fired. Blood splattered against the bedpost. Shocked by her own display of violence, Amber sprinted down the steps and ordered her daughter to go to her neighbor's and stay there.

"If it wasn't for my daughter, I would have committed suicide years ago," Amber said. "Some of the mental torture will never leave me the rest of my life. It was so severe, it will be with me every day."

Amber then called the police and told them what she did.

"It's hard for us to justify shooting somebody who's asleep in the bed," Sheriff Jeffrey Trafton said. "But when we arrived she looked more like a victim than a killer."

"She was in a state of shock," Orange said. "She had finally taken action to free herself from years of abuse. The state, of course, cannot let such a deed go unchecked."

A CONSPIRACY AFOOT?

As police investigated the murder scene, they discovered another James Cummings secret.

He was gathering materials to make a "dirty bomb."

Fueled by his white supremacist ideology, James planned to go to Washington, D.C for Barack Obama's presidential inauguration. Once there, he would set off his dirty bomb.

"He had all the ingredients inside the garage," Orange said. "The FBI found the instructions for the dirty bomb. There were four 1-gallon containers with uranium, thorium and beryllium powder. There were numerous other jugs which contained lithium metal, thermite, magnesium ribbon, black iron oxide and other explosive substances. James Cummings meant business and there is clear evidence he was going to follow through on his plan. Whether he could have pulled it off is another story."

Had his plan gone to fruition, James could have potentially killed hundreds of people.

Amber saved not only herself but innumerable lives by killing James herself.

"The stuff that he had wasn't dangerous," Bangor Police Chief Jeffrey Trafton said. "In its present form, it wasn't dangerous to the community. Technicians told me what you had to do, you had to get real close for a long period of time before it would have any effect as far as the radioactivity. When the stuff was found, obviously detectives from the state police came and we didn't know what it was. But there was no danger to the community. That was established fairly quickly. But my involvement since it was handed over to the state police has been little to none."

THE TRIAL

Amber would remain in a state of shock after the murder. She worried more about her daughter's well-being than her own. She was fully prepared to go to jail.

"Her mental state was still askew after she killed James," Orange said. "She probably saw prison as a welcome respite from her abusive life. She had been in 'prison' already and saw the jail system as a safe place."

Amber would plead guilty during trial proceedings. Her story would make the media rounds, however, and she soon found numerous supporters in her small Maine town. People showed up wearing "Free Amber" t-shirts.

"There was no way in hell a jury in that vicinity would have found her guilty," Orange said. "None."

Amber seemed to have found leniency on both sides of the judicial system. Her attorney and the prosecutors would come up with a plea deal which called for a sentence of up to eight years but with Amber serving no less than a year. This would be followed by six years of probation.

Her attorney then recommended to the judge that Amber spend no whatsoever behind bars while the Assistant Attorney General, Leane Zania, wanted Cummings to spend a year in jail.

"This kind of 'self-help' is severely anti-social behavior," Zania wrote. "It will be punished accordingly."

During the course of the trial, Amber would not take the stand in her defense. Three mental health experts who had counseled her after the killing all affirmed the fact that Amber had endured traumatic abuse. They advised the judge not to send her to jail.

The psychiatrists had given Amber a diagnosis of "shared psychotic disorder" which in layman's terms meant that she had absorbed some of his craziness just by being around him.

"You don't hang out by the outhouse without getting a rash," Orange said. "So that is how Amber was able to endure all of that psychological trauma. She became so desensitized to it that it became the norm after a few years."

The judge sentenced her to eight years in prison but it was a suspended sentence, allowing her to go free.

"The terrible thing is, I was forced to take the life of someone that I loved very much to save my daughter that I love very much," Amber said. "It's something that I will have to live with for the rest of my life, and it won't be easy. I'll always wonder. I'll always be looking over my shoulder, always wondering if he can come back from the dead."

In her public remarks, Amber requested that the community forgive her husband and not have any anger toward him.

"I just want to thank the community and people of Maine," Amber said after leaving the courtroom. "Because without them, I don't think my daughter and I could have made all this progress. Really, really wonderful caring people. If I was anywhere else, we wouldn't be doing this well. I believe that with all my heart."

"The people around here are pretty incredible. They gave me the benefit of the doubt, and a chance to prove myself. There was a lot of support, an unbelievable amount of support, in Belfast. People came out and took care of us and made sure we had everything we need."

Amber stated that after she shot James that she fell into a "state of shock and numbness." She would continue to dream about James, having nightmares about him choking her.

Since then, she dedicated herself to trying to undo the mental damage James did to her daughter.

"I hope to raise a really good kid, who cares a lot about people," Amber said. I hope she ends up strong and can take care of herself. I think she will."

DEATH ROW GRANNY

It never ends.

No way.

No way am I letting this man demean and degrade me another day.

He's just like my father.

A binge drinker. And the binges were happening more and more.

He's on the road to nowhere and taking me with him.

It never ends.

First my father. Now him.

Fuck it.

I threw the cigarette on the blanket. I knew it was flammable.

Then I watched the smoke rise and smiled.

In Lumberton, North Carolina, Thomas Burke fell victim to a house fire which was caused by a burning cigarette. Investigative authorities thought that he had fallen asleep while smoking, leaving thirty-eight-year-old Velma Burke as his widow.

They didn't know that the fire was set by Velma.

Velma knew how to play the part of the grieving widow. She cried and gave the authorities the requisite crocodile tears. No one would believe that the murder of Thomas Burke would set off a series of killings performed by the seemingly kind and harmless church-going woman with the soft voice.

EARLY LIFE

Velma Bullard grew up as the second of nine children in the rural part of Sampson County, North Carolina.

Times were tough for the Bullard family. They would live on a small farm with no electricity, running water or an outhouse.

"They had to go outdoors," forensic psychologist Paula Orange said. "The entire family had to endure the indignity of going into the woods or using pots to shit and piss."

The home was small and cramped for the nine children. Velma would be forced to sleep in the same bedroom with her parents until the age of five.

Her father was a loom repairman (fixing an apparatus that was used to weave clothing) and an abusive alcoholic. Velma had an older brother, Olive, who were subject to his nightly beatings. Lillie, her mother, was too meek to protect her children from her husband's violent outbursts.

"She had the type of father who would not need any provocation," Orange said. "He would take out the pettiest frustrations, like not being able to find something around the house, and take it out on the children. Velma would become resentful toward her mother who was too weak or indifferent to stop her father from beating on the kids. She accepted his discipline as 'the way it was.'"

Velma would find school as a welcome escape from her dreadful home life. She loved her teacher and was an excellent student during her early grade school years. When she would return home from school, she took solace in the fact that her father would always arrive home late as he worked long hours at the textile mill.

"Her father Murphy had that Protestant work ethic in him," Orange said. "He accepted the long hours and low pay, seeing a kind of nobility in that. Only problem was, he would binge drink. Not store bought alcohol but homemade moonshine. After a couple of shots, he would be 'lit' and inflict his wrath on everyone in the house."

By the age of eleven, Velma would be forced to take on various chores around the farm. She would clean up the house, washing and iron everyone's clothing (eleven people). Her father would chastise her for not mending or sewing his work clothes properly as well.

"Her father was a stern taskmaster," Orange said. "Hell, you can say 'slave driver.' He would have Velma come home early from school days when the laundry got too backed up. Velma hated this and felt embarrassed. Her family didn't have much and as she grew older her classmates began to see her for what she was, a poor girl that was an easy mark for teasing."

Velma would grow to be 5'3" but gain weight as she got older. She would be mocked about her obesity, her shoddy clothes the gap between her two front teeth. She would also be called "knot head" after she ran head first into a boy at school which left a permanent contusion on her forehead.

By the age of twelve,Velma seemed to have taken on all of her mother's duties. She would cook all of the family meals in addition to performing cleaning around the farm house. She would miss school for days at a time as her father forced her to complete chores around the home before she could continue her education.

"Academic achievement was not at the forefront of her father's mind," Orange said. "Her mother was of little use because of her depression and mental illness. Velma was the oldest girl so she took on the duties of mom at an age where she should have been playing with dolls."

ANGER, ABUSE, AND CHURCH

Despite her father's verbal abuse and alcohol-fueled beatings, the family kept up a face of religious interest. Velma would be sent to Bible school every year until the age of thirteen. During her last year of Bible school, her father marked the occasion by buying Velma a silk pink dress with ribbons. Velma recalled the day as one of the happiest of her life.

The happiness would be short-lived.

Velma would claim that her father raped her when she was thirteen years old. She revealed this only to her pastor in her later years before she stood trial. Velma did not even tell her mother whom she did not think would believe the molestation took place.

"Things that went on inside our home when I grew up," Velma said. "Were kept inside."

At the age of fifteen, Velma continued to excel in school. Despite her chubby physique, she becomes adept at basketball and is pegged to be the team's star player for the upcoming season. But her father did not allow her to play.

"Who is going to iron these damn clothes?" he snarled.

The family then moved to Robeson county and switched from the Presbyterian denomination to Baptist. It was here that Velma would meet Thomas Burke and the two made it clear that they wanted to date. Once again, Velma's father would intervene, telling Velma that she had to wait until her sixteenth birthday until she could date.

The two waited patiently for her birthday to arrive and the following year Thomas would propose to her while they went to the movies.

Knowing that her father would not approve, Velma and Thomas eloped, moving to Dillon, South Carolina. Neither Thomas or Velma had any money as they both quit high school to get married. Thomas then went to work at a local textile mill.

"At this point, I believe that Velma began to realize that her life would not be that much better with Thomas," Orange said. "He literally has the same job as her father."

Economics forced Velma and Thomas to move in with his parents. This arrangement would last for a year until Thomas got a better paying job at a soft drink company.

At the age of nineteen, Velma would give birth to her first son, Ronnie. The couple would then move back to Parkton, North Carolina where they would remain in the same home for eleven years. Two years later, the young couple would welcome a daughter named Kim.

A CYCLE OF RELIGION AND ABUSE

The Burkes would be fixtures at the local Baptist church with Velma taking the reigns to teach a Sunday school class. But the prayers and sermons would do little to offset the growing ennui in the Burke home. Two years after giving birth to Kim, Velma would get hit by a drunk driver while crossing the street. She would be hospitalized for an extended period, suffering both physically and mentally.

Thomas' job at the soft drink company would not be enough to provide for the family. Velma would be forced to leave her small children at home and work in a textile mill just like her father. The couple would have different work hours, with Velma working nights and Thomas working days as they would take turns watching the children.

Velma would fall victim to the hard work at the mill and the stress of raising two young children. She began bleeding and her doctor performed a hysterectomy.

Velma's mother would take pity on the couple and give them one acre of land near their old farm. Thomas would build a three-bedroom home for the family but Velma was already going down a slippery slope. Her personality changed after the hysterectomy, claiming that she always felt "nervous and afraid."

Things would get worse as Thomas suffered a head injury in a car accident. He then began to drink heavily and begin to beat Velma.

"It was deja vu," Orange said. "Velma had, in essence, married her father."

One night, the couple argued and Thomas punched Velma in an alcohol-fueled tantrum. The police are called to the home and Velma sent Thomas to the state hospital to get treatment for his drinking. Her husband remains there for three days but when he returns home, his behavior is worse than behavior. He's angry at Velma for sending him to the "drunk tank". His alcoholism worsens and he would go on to lose his job because of absenteeism.

"Velma is thirty-five years old at this time," Orange said. "But she's an old thirty-five with crow's feet under her eyes and a hangdog look. She's had a rough life, not necessarily by her own design, and it has taken its toll."

Velma leaves the textile mill but then finds two different jobs in order to support the family. During the day, she works as a sales clerk in a Belk department store. At night, she goes to work as a machine operator in a cotton mill.

Thomas, meanwhile, would continue to drink.

He rages on a daily basis, on one occasion he pinned son Ronnie up against the wall and threatened him with a knife. Velma would faint during the encounter and be transported to the hospital. She was diagnosed as having a nervous breakdown and lapsed into a serious depression. The medical staff gave her tranquilizers to calm down. Velma believed that it was during this stint in the hospital that she became addicted to the painkillers.

"The drugs were helping," Orange said. "When nothing else did. So she wanted more and more."

Velma's children acknowledged that their mother's mood swings were due to the drugs.

Over the next three years, Velma would go in and out of the hospital for drug overdoses. After each visit, her addiction only grew as did her prescription list.

"She fell through the cracks in her own family," Orange said. "And in the system itself. Her family had their own issues to deal with as Thomas would abuse everyone on a daily basis. Finally, Velma did something she could control. She killed her husband."

On April 21st, 1969, Velma would drop a cigarette on the floor of her home and waited until her husband inhaled enough smoke to die.

His death, however, would do nothing to solve Velma's problems.

Her addictions and anxiety would only get worse.

A HOSPITAL FREQUENT FLYER

Velma would have another nervous breakdown after killing Thomas and lapse into a guilt-ridden depression. But seven months later, a co-worker at the Belk department store would introduce her to fifty-four-year-old Jennings Barfield. Jennings had emphysema and diabetes but Velma would marry him anyway. Unlike her marriage with Thomas which started out well, Velma's marriage with the older Jennings would be troubled from the start. Her drug addiction would escalate and Jennings would express his own regret at marrying her.

"I don't know why I married her," Jennings said. "All she does is pop pills all day."

After less than three years of marriage, Velma decided to part ways with Jennings. She didn't file for divorce, however, she decided to poison him with arsenic. She would later claim that she only meant to "make him sick."

Jennings Barfield was already ill and doctors had no suspicion that Velma was behind the death. Arsenic was a slow burn poison that could kill without detection. The autopsy called for no arsenic test and Velma had gotten away with murder once again.

But Seven months later, Velma would overdose on her prescription meds and become hospitalized. Her family recognized the pattern but could not wean Velma off of the drinks. She would remain hospitalized for three weeks.

Her personality seemed to change after the hospital release. She returned to work at Belk department store but kept being combative and argumentative with customers. Her boss knew of her circumstances and tried to coax her to do better. He took her away from the public contact and into the back stock room where he had her put pricing on the clothing items.

Her boss soon realized that Velma's addiction had gotten out of control. Velma would not be able to function in the back room, leaving tasks uncompleted as she would have her prescription medications delivered to the store.

"It is a hopeless situation," the store manager told Velma's son Ronnie before he fired his mother.

BROKE AND DESTITUTE

With no income, Velma would lose the family home as she no longer paid the mortgage. She would be forced to move back in with her parents and face the two people she blamed everything for.

Her father had grown ill, however, and would die from lung cancer shortly after Velma moved back into the home. She would feel bad about her father's death and admit that she had a love/hate relationship with him.

"I had learned to love him as much as I had hated him," Velma said. "He was so good to my kids. I think he tried to do with my kids like he wished he had done to us. He could not stand to see me correct them. If I would pick them up and spank them, he would ask me, 'Isn't that enough?'"

But after her father's death Velma self-medicated once again. She overdosed and was hospitalized for two weeks. Her family didn't judge, they instead thought she was "cursed."

"Velma needed psychiatric help," Orange said. "So she began medicating herself with deleterious results. She would "doctor shop" for different physicians who would be manipulated into giving her the drugs she wanted. Her addiction eventually grows until she becomes desperate for money in order to fuel the drug habit."

A MURDERER AND A THIEF

Velma began stealing from those closest to her, starting with her mother. Her mother confronted Velma about a missing check and Velma went ballistic.

"She had violent mood swings," Orange said. "The medication had completely changed her personality as she needed the drugs above all else. The people around her were not familiar with how to handle a person who had this kind of mental illness. So this made for a very dangerous cocktail for her and anyone close to her."

Hitting a new low, Velma took out a $1,000 loan under her mother Lillie's name. She put up the family home as collateral and forged her mother's signature on the documents. Velma then blew through the money and a month later took out another loan, once again using her mother's house as collateral. The following month, she emptied the checking account on her now deceased husband, Jennings. Two months later, the loan company began sending Velma overdue notices as she had not been paying off the loan.

"In Velma's mind," Orange said. "She had no other choice but to kill off her own mother."

Velma went to the local pharmacy and looked for bottles that had the warning of "fatal if ingested." She put the poison into a drink for her mother and watched as she drank the fatal elixir.

Her mother then began vomiting and lost control of her bowels. Within a few hours, her mother could not so much as walk and an ambulance was called.

Velma came to visit her in the hospital to finish the job. Armed with a Thermos, she made a special concoction of chicken soup and arsenic.

"Drink it slow," Velma said as she tenderly lifted the cups to the lips of her ailing mother. "Slow."

Her mother would eventually die of "natural causes" as no one suspected Velma of committing murder. Instead, she received sympathy.

"So sorry for your loss," hospital staff said.

"The thing with arsenic is that it shuts down the whole system," Orange said. "So hospital staff just chalked up her mother's weakness to old age. Checking for arsenic poisoning would be the furthest thing from their mind."

Velma showed the necessary emotion and received sympathy from friends and family. She then moved in with her daughter Kim and son-in-law Dennis who lived in a trailer park. She could not evade the authorities for long though as the authorities caught wind of Velma's check forgeries.

Velma reacted as she always did. She would run away and medicate herself.

"Her drug addiction kept pushing her into a corner and she saw no way out," Orange said. "So, this time, she goes to her son Ronnie's house and overdoses again, trying to kill herself. She falls and breaks her collar bone which laid her out in the hospital another three weeks."

But the police find her situation unsympathetic.

"We're sorry, Velma," the deputy informed her at her hospital bed. "But once you have been cleared for release, we will arrest you."

Velma would not have that. She tried to overdose again but this go around the hospital staff pumped out her stomach.

She was sent to court the next day and sentenced to six months in jail for the forgery. She is released after four months for good behavior.

NO REHAB HERE

Her addiction still unchecked, Velma returned to live with Kim and her son-in-law. She rummaged through the belongings of her son-in-law and stole a check, forging his name so she can get more prescription meds. Her daughter Kim now has caught wind of her mother's addiction, pleading with her doctors to stop prescribing her.

"In some ways," Orange said. "The doctors were just as guilty as she was. But back in the day, there was no way to cross-reference this stuff like we do now. Once she had her fill with one doctor she would go to the next and the next."

Velma's addiction prevented her from taking a forty-hour a week job. So she looked for alternative forms of income.

She would find a job taking care of the elderly.

Montgomery and Dolly Edwards would be her first clients.

"She found herself some easy targets," Orange said. "There didn't seem to be any legislative body in place that prevents sociopaths from caretaking the elderly. So Velma doesn't slip through any cracks, she just befriends the elderly couple and begins taking care of them."

Montgomery was blind and unable to walk. He was 93-years old and his 83-year old wife was too feeble to take care of him. They paid $75 a week for Velma to become their live-in caretaker.

All was good, at least in the beginning. But Dolly had a sharp tongue and would criticize Velma daily. Velma would keep a nice exterior unless confronted, saw Dolly has yet another wheel in her cycle of verbal abuse.

"It seemed to be a never-ending loop for her," Orange said. "Being forced to deal with verbally abusive people. Velma had long since snapped and Dollie simply had no idea who she was dealing with."

Velma began to plot out Montgomery and Dollie's demise until she meets their nephew, Stuart Taylor.

Stuart was already married but was blown away when he met the caretaker of his Aunt Dollie.

Velma would play it cool, stealing what she could from the couple in terms of petty cash and household items that had value. They outlived their usefulness to her within a year as Montgomery died of "natural causes". One month later, Dolly also passed away.

And again, no one suspected the sweet and soft-spoken Velma to have had anything to do with their deaths.

MOVING ON

Velma saw being a caretaker as a perfect front for her. She could steal as much money as she could and when the old folks detected something amiss she would simply poison them. After killing the Edwards' couple, she set the word out at church that she as available to be a caregiver. The pastor would refer her to Margie Lee Pittman who was seeking for a caregiver for her elderly parents, John Henry and Record Lee.

"She comes here twice a week," the pastor reassured Pittman. "She's a nice, kindly woman. You can't go wrong."

Pittman's father, John Henry Lee, was eighty years old when he discovered that his new caregiver had forged a $50 check on his account. He then fell violently ill, suffering through a spastic spell of vomiting, diarrhea, and convulsions. The doctors would chalk up his quick death to gastroenteritis but in fact, he had been poisoned with arsenic.

Velma played the caregiver role until his end. She attended his funeral and cried with the family, sending an ornate wreath (with money stolen from the dead man) to the proceedings.

For whatever reason, Velma spared Lee's wife and moved back to Lumberton, North Carolina to live in a trailer park. She began working as an aide in a nursing home and received word from Stuart that he was now a widow. The two began dating and she moved part of her belongings into his home.

"Stuart is a nice guy," Orange said. "He has no idea what kind of woman Velma is. She is so manipulative and cunning that the younger man is putty in her hands. So the relationship starts great as she reels him in with kindness and charm."

The couple are happy cohabitating until Stuart Stuart finds a letter addressed to Velma from the state penitentiary.

Curious, he began reading the correspondence and realized that is from a former cellmate of Velma.

Stuart became enraged. He threatened to "expose" Velma to all of his family and friends. Somehow, someway, however, she was able to calm him down.

He then found out that she had forged over $200 in checks on his account. The two argued but stayed together for the next two months.

"Velma had the Christian facade down pat," Orange said. "She asked Stuart to forgive her and the next thing you know they are going to a Rex Humbard revival. But before they went, she poured arsenic poison in both his beer and tea. She made sure he drank every drop."

Returning home from the revival, Stuart started to vomit on the drive home, the poison kicking in.

Velma had to keep the con going. She had to appear like a concerned girlfriend so she called up Stuart's daughter, Alice, later that night and told her that Stuart had came down with the flu.

Stuart's daughter expressed concern but Velma kept her at bay.

"Don't you worry now, honey. I'll take care of everything."

Stuart died the next day.

Velma would speak at Stuart's funeral and tearfully asked for his wedding band. His family graciously allowed her to have it and gave her $400 to help her cope with the grief.

But Alice knew her father was a picture of health. She vociferously argued for more tests beyond the standard autopsy and sure enough, arsenic had been found in Stuart's tissues.

On March 10th, 1978, the sheriffs arrived at Velma's home to bring her in for questioning. She was interrogated for over three hours, holding her ground. But she knows the evidence will trump her denials and tries to commit suicide after being released. This go around, however, her son Ronnie stopped her.

The sheriffs come to visit Velma again and she has one more surprise up her sleeve.

But Velma has one more surprise up her sleeve.

She would confess. Not only for the murder of Stuart but of six others.

"I set my first husband on fire," Velma confessed without an attorney present. "And I killed the rest of them."

"It was almost as if she wanted to be free of the guilt she had been carrying," Orange said. "Her confession seemed to take a burden off her back."

"The last ten years were like that," Velma said. "A drug nightmare. It was a case of not knowing where you are or what you've done."

The bodies of her victims were later exhumed and all tested positive for arsenic.

FACING THE GRIM REAPER

Velma's case would be prosecuted by Joe Freeman Britt, who was listed in the Guinness Book of World Records as the country's "deadliest prosecutor."

Velma would plead not guilty by reason of insanity but the court denied her plea.

"I needed to keep them sick until I could pay back the money I had stolen from them," Velma said. "I wanted to earn their thanks by nursing them back to health. I needed the money. I was addicted to pain killers. Anti-depressants. Amphetamines."

On November 23rd, 1978, Velma's trial would begin in Elizabethtown, North Carolina where she would be charged with the first-degree murder of her boyfriend, Stuart Taylor. The trial lasted seven days and the jury reached a verdict of guilty, placing her on death row at the age of 47. She was scheduled to be executed on February 3rd, 1979 but received a stay.

Velma would be sentenced to death and the verdict was appealed all the way to the U.S. Supreme court. Her attorney maintained that the jury had never been presented with the full extent of Velma's "addiction and background." Velma remained tight-lipped about that to everyone but her pastor. Her attorney felt thought her horrific background could have been used as part of her defense and the jury would have found her to be more of a sympathetic case.

CHANGING SPOTS?

"She's not the same person who went to prison in 1978," Kim Burke Norton, Velma's daughter said.

While in jail, Velma became a model prisoner.

"The first week I was here was the worst week," Velma recalled. "Everything about it."

Velma no longer had access to her drugs in prison and she began to dry out. With daily visits from two different pastors, Velma began to discuss her anger and repressed issues that fueled her addiction and murders.

Velma would claim that as she was awaiting trial in 1978 she came to a "meeting with Christ" that caused her to "change inwardly."

Velma heard a broadcast by radio evangelist JK Kinkle. "Jesus loves you, prisoners, too," Kinkle said. "He died for you too. No matter what you've done, the Lord will forgive you."

After Velma heard this sermon, she dropped to her knees and cried out to God.

She would then become the "go to" counselor for young inmates in the prison.

The inmates would nickname Velma as "Mama Margie" because of her wisdom and she would in turn think of them as her "adopted children."

The prison guards and counselors would take the most incorrigible prisoners and place them in a cell next to Velma. Velma would invariably counsel the young prisoner and advise them on the correct path.

"They'd come in ready to kill themselves," Sister Mary Teresa Floyd said. "And here she was with a death sentence, mothering and helping them."

"Living in prison is a struggle," Velma said. "Even at its best. And I know that without Him and His strength that has sustained me, I couldn't have made it even this far."

Her stay on death row soon became a part of the news brief. During this time, a phalanx of evangelists would take her cause to the mainstream. The Reverend Hugh Hoyle would become Velma's personal minister as she received stays of execution in September, October and December of 1981. She would also have a letter correspondence with Ruth Graham, Billy Graham's wife as well as meeting their daughter Ann.

While Velma impressed the Christian do-gooders, the family members of the victims were not taken in by her "conversion."

"She's got religion now, they say," Margie Lee Pittman said. "Well, she had religion before. So we all thought."

A few more stays were granted until 1984 when the U.S. Supreme Court justice Warren Burger granted her a stay until August of that year. At this point, however, her execution seemed inevitable. In an ironic move, Velma would choose poison rather than the gas chamber and enjoyed the final visits from her children and grandchildren.

During the final week before her execution, the Reverend Hoyle, and his wife came to the prison with a battery-powered portable keyboard. His wife played the little organ then the Reverend sang "He Hideth My Soul" and "He is So precious to Me" in the cramped visitor booth.

Velma sang along, whistling in the graveyard before the reaper came for her.

She then wrote letters to each of the victim's family asking them for forgiveness. Reverend Hoyle would deliver the letters to the families, all of whom would refuse them.

MEET THE HANGMAN

As her execution date neared, Velma was placed in a solitary cell that stood directly across from the death chamber.

"It's total isolation," Velma said. "From everyone I had been with for six years."

North Carolina Governor James B.Hunt would reject her final plea for clemency.

On the day of her execution, the jail house would turn into a media frenzy. Death penalty advocates gathered outside the prison and chanted "Hip, hip, hurrah...K-I-L-L" while some sloganeered with "burn, bitch, burn". The protesters held up a few placards that quote

Romans ch.13 which ironically was a verse that Velma would repeat to guards during her prison stay.

"For rulers are not a terror to good works, but to the evil...(The ruler) beareth no the sword in vain, for he is the minister of God, a revenger to execute wrath upon him that doeth evil."

The execution was scheduled to take place at 2:00 a.m but the protesters remained outside, their chants reduced to a simple "Kill her! Kill her!"

On November 2nd, 1984, Velma would be executed by lethal injection. The prison official came out and addressed the press, giving out copies of Barfield's statement of apology. The reporters then eagerly anticipated what Velma requested for her last meal. Initially, Velma just wanted the normally scheduled prison food; chicken livers, collard greens and a sheet cake with peanut butter icing. The last meal was delivered but Velma immediately lost her appetite. Instead, she opted for Cheese Doodles and a glass of Coca-Cola.

"Her attorney believed that Velma could have done some good in life," Orange said. "He stated that she could have become a teacher, counselor or a pastor. But her father set her on a path of self-destruction that she couldn't escape from. By the time she the left that road to ruin, she was too far gone in terms of her murderous acts. Justice had to be served in the end. In the end, the law doesn't care how genuine you are in your pleas for forgiveness. It only cares about the rule of law."

"I'm sorry for the hurt that I've caused," Velma said before her execution. "So many people, today if it were possible, I wish I could take every bit of hurt on myself."

KILLER BABE : THE TRUE STORY OF BRITTANY HOLBERG

65

Brittany Holberg was a twenty-three years old prostitute when she was convicted of murdering 80-year-old A.B. Towery Jr, stabbing him over sixty times.

The controversy surrounding the case centered around the relationship of Brittany and Towery prior to the killing. Brittany argued that Towery was a client who went into a rage when he found drugs on her person. He attacked her and she retaliated in self-defense.

Further investigation would reveal otherwise, however, as Brittany would use numerous household items in a brutal assault on the elderly man.

She fled the scene only to be caught at a McDonald's after police received a tip from a witness who saw her on "America's Most Wanted."

With her good looks and well-proportioned body, Brittany has remained in the spotlight as she was featured in a Maxim Magazine article as one of the "hottest women on death row".

Brittany still sits on death row today with her case being appealed on the numerous levels in the court system.

EARLY LIFE

Brittany was born on January 1, 1973, in Amarillo, Texas.

Accounts on Brittany's home life vary as she would manipulate according to the needs of her listener. To her probation officer, she informed them that her home life was "good" and that she "had everything that she ever wanted". She would often describe her mother as her best friend.

During other occasions, however, Brittany would paint a different story.

She would describe her parents as being "hippie-drugsters". Brittany would state that she was close to her mother but never knew her father, a heroin addict who was in and out of the Texas prison system. Her mother would later marry a man named John Schwartz with the couple marrying and divorcing four times.

They would drink heavily and openly smoke weed in front of the young Brittany who would be sexually assaulted by a babysitter at the age of five. When she was twelve, one of her aunts was murdered and according to Brittany "everything fell apart" at home. Her parents would leave her unattended as they indulged in pot and booze.

"They just stopped working," Brittany said. "They just let everything go."

She would be gang raped by two men who confronted her in an alley behind her home when she was thirteen.

Brittany would then spend the majority of her time living with her grandmother. By the age of sixteen, however, she would run away with her boyfriend Ward. The two would make it as far as California, get married, and have a young daughter named Mackenzie.

The union would not last long, however. Brittany would divorce Ward and move back to her native Amarillo. Ward would take Mackenzie and move to Tulsa, Oklahoma.

Brittany would state that she suffered a knee injury and would become addicted to pain medication during treatment. She would then graduate to harder drugs like cocaine.

In and out of rehab, Brittany's life spiraled out of control. She could manipulate with the best of them, however, and would escape from the Midland Halfway House with the help of a female counselor.

Brittany would hang out with the drug-using crowd and her own habits were out of control. To support her addiction, Brittany began working as a prostitute.

This would put her in harm's way on many an occasion as she would get gang-raped and beaten severely.

The assault would put her in the hospital but she would resume "tricking" when she was released.

"At that point in her life, Brittany was incorrigible," forensic psychologist Paula Orange said."Numerous people had reached to her and tried to help. She had extended family members trying to help. Friends trying to help. Even church outreach workers. All to no avail. The drugs had taken root and she was dead set on manipulating everyone around her. Family, roommates, church members, doctors, dentists, and pharmacists would all fall victim to her schemes to get drugs."

By 1993, Brittany was a full-blown drug-addicted prostitute with the rap sheet to prove it. In April of that year, she would steal a gun from her step-father. She then passed over $1300 in "hot" checks and applied for several store credit cards using a fake name.

Brittany and one of her aunts would run a scam on dentists, lying to them about their pain levels in order to get prescription medication. When the prescription drugs ran out, she would return to street drugs like cocaine and heroin. Arrests would follow and Brittany would be charged in Hale County with drug possession, paraphernalia, and public intoxication.

Upon her release, Brittany would proceed to steal her mother's car and forge checks in her name. The prostitution continued unabated as well as she stole the wallet from one of her "tricks" who pressed charges.

While in jail for the theft, Brittany would be introduced to Ella Gibbs and Patricia Karnes who ran the ministry in the Randall County Jail. The women tried to get Brittany on the right track and introduce her to Christianity.

"I wanted to reassure Brittany that she is a valuable person, that her life has great potential, and that this is the mortal portion of an eternal life," Karnes said. " Brittany is an eternal being and through the many prayers from my [prayer] group [in Lubbock,] I have been led to come back into this child's life to support her here, to encourage her, to find her courage from the Holy Spirit within her, and to let her know that there is a human being mortal person who will stand beside her and see the good in her and support whatever God plans for the rest of your [sic] life."

A.B. TOWERY

Towery was by all accounts a nice man. His son would bristle at the idea that he was Brittany's "sugar daddy".

"Dad wasn't a dirty old man," his son said. "Dad was just trying to help somebody and look what he got, and now she's getting three meals a day and a warm place to sleep."

The defense would later bring up the fact that he once pulled a knife on his son Russell during a temper tantrum. Towery would have a history with prostitutes (according to court testimony). Connie Baker would be a prostitute from the 1980s to 1997 and stated that Towery was one of her clients. Baker would also claim Tower as a client but she also had a history of drug possession and auto theft. Diana Wheeler would also admit to being one of Towery's prostitutes in the years of 1994 and 1995. She had come to his home and he even went so far as to clean the stains off his Mel Mac dinnerware. But Wheeler also had a long criminal history like Baker, arrested for prostitution, criminal trespass and giving false identification to a police officer.

The controversy at the trial was if Brittany and Towery had an ongoing "sex-for-money" relationship.

This would be vigorously discounted by family members.

His daughter-in-law would come to the home and help with some housekeeping. His sons would also visit daily and never report any "ladies of the evening" coming to visit their father.

The picture just didn't fit.

Brittany stated she was sent to Towery's place by a fellow streetwalker who went by the moniker of "Green Eyes" but that it was later revealed that no such prostitute by that name existed. Brittany had lied like she had so many times before.

The two seemed to have met by chance.

COMING BACK FROM THE GROCERY STORE

November 13th, 1996 was another normal day for the 80-year old A.B Towery. He had just purchased groceries at an Albertson's store and was walking back to his apartment. As he entered the courtyard, he was approached by the 23-year old Brittany Holberg.

She asked to use his telephone and Towery consented. He wanted to help the sweet-voiced Brittany and didn't believe that she posed any kind of physical threat to him.

What he didn't know was that Brittany was coming down from a cocaine high and had not slept in ten days.

"Brittany could be persuasive," Orange said. "She was well-versed in how to charm people, she knew exactly what to say and do in terms of body language. She was like a trained actress. It didn't take much cajoling on her part to convince Towery to let her inside his home. He probably thought 'what's the big deal?'"

Once inside, Brittany would demand money from the elderly man but he refused. Brittany then attacked Towery, trying to strong arm the wallet out of his pocket. The struggle began in the living room. The two then pushed and pulled each other around a partition that separated the kitchen from the living room. They then returned to the living room. At some point, Towery tried to leave the apartment but Brittany pulled him back in. The evidence also indicated that the two paused during this 45-minute fight, catching their breath and nursing their wounds. Brittany would sustain minor stab wounds to her stomach and thigh.

"This was most likely a fight that had a lot of clutching and grabbing," Orange said. "There was less blood in the living room so the conjecture is that is where the fight started. There was blood near the door so that suggests that Towery was bleeding out and trying to escape for help. Remember, he was a slow-moving 80-year old man. Brittany was a young woman but she was fueled by cocaine. He's getting tired a lot faster than she will."

Eventually, Brittany gained the upper hand. She used various objects around the home to beat down Towery. She started with a cast iron frying pan, then a steam iron, a claw hammer, a fruit knife, a butcher knife and then two forks. Towery would fall to the floor, a bloody mess.

Brittany then took a lamp and shoved its base five inches down his throat which choked him to death.

Satisfied that he had finally killed Tower, Brittany removed her bloody clothes. She washed up in his bathroom then went to his closet to find some clothes that fit her.

Walking back to his dead body, Brittany retrieved the wallet out of Towery's pocket. She took out the $1400 dollars he had and dropped the now empty wallet onto his stomach.

Brittany casually walked out of the apartment and hitched a ride with a young couple. The couple dropped her off at a local crack house where Brittany paid them off with two $100 bills (which had blood stains on them). Inside the drug den, Brittany befriended the proprietor and changed clothes again. She then went to a local hotel with hundreds of dollars worth of cocaine and indulged.

TRIAL

Brittany's defense attorney, Catherine Brown Dodson, would argue that Holberg acted in self-defense when she killed Towery. Her primary argument was that Towery was far from an innocent, elderly man. He was, in fact, a drug abuser himself who became physically violent with Brittany when he found a crack pipe on her person. He then hit Brittany two times in the head when she turned her back to him. Brittany retaliated and ultimately put the lamp post in his mouth in an attempt to end the fight.

Brittany then fled as she believed that no one would believe her side of the story because she was both a prostitute and a drug addict.

While in jail, Brittany would try to coerce Katina Dixon, her cellmate to kill Vickie Marie Kirkpatrick who was the prosecution witness.

Towery's history with prostitutes would be brought up in court testimony. They would also mention incidents of violence with his ex-wife and children but jurors didn't believe the old man was in any type of shape to employ the service of a prostitute.

"My father didn't even like the word 'sex'", one of his sons said. "He was old-fashioned."

A psychiatrist would testify, however, that Brittany had battered wife syndrome, post-traumatic stress disorder, and cocaine addiction.

The jury did not take long to deliberate, finding Brittany to be a cunning, manipulative liar who committed one of the most brutal crimes in the history of Amarillo.

They would find her guilty and Brittany would be moved to death row at Gatesville, Texas.

"I can't even explain to you," Brittany said in a magazine interview. "What it's like to have someone say 'You are sentenced to die.' It's words. You feel helpless, numb. It's almost as if your emotions shut you down."

Brittany would spend her first few weeks in prison laying prone on her bed in a zombie-like state. Over time, she grew accepting of her situation. She knew she was going to die but made it a point to learn to take each day one step at a time.

Her inspiration for cleaning up her act came from the memory of her daughter Mackenzie.

"I cannot live," Brittany said. "And I cannot die, knowing that my child has to live with the horror that these people tried to say about me, the story of the crime, their depiction that I was a cold-blooded person."

Brittany states that she dedicates her days to reading, writing to family and working on her law appeals. She also is anti-death penalty advocate.

She would follow other Texas inmates who were now on death row and make appeals on their behalf, specifically that of Betty Lou Beets.

"I realized," Brittany said. "It doesn't matter whether I'm guilty or innocent, this has now become a very political thing... At this point, they're just killing to kill."

She complained that after a recent jail uprising, the treatment of death row inmates has worsened.

"You would not believe the treatment we are given," Brittany said. "Just two weeks ago, we were informed that not only would we be strip-searched for our one hour of recreation a day, but also when taken for a shower. So for the last two weeks, we have been stripped no less than six times a day. This is every day, sometimes at times like 2:30-3 a.m., and we never leave the building or our cells for that matter."

As of this writing, Brittany's stay of execution has been appealed and appealed for the past eighteen years.

Her attorneys would exhaust the appeal process in the state system but it is now in the federal courts.

Her case, however, has been costing taxpayers "conservatively to be at least $400,000" according to county criminal attorney James Farren. In the future, he has decided to forgo seeking the death penalty in capital cases.

Farren continues to favor a death penalty but only under certain circumstances like "a guy walks into a day care center and kills the children or if someone kills a police officer or a firefighter in the line of duty."

Farren predicted that Brittany would remain on death row for another five years at least. "They can go through the U.S District Court in Amarillo, then it can go to the Fifth U.S Circuit Court and the U.S. Supreme Court. Then from there it can go back to the U.S. District."

But the appeals can come to a halt if the district judge refuses to hear it again.

"If the Supreme Court says 'no'," Farren said. "That's when the district judge can feel safe in stopping this process."

The entire process has been an infuriating one for the Towery family. His son both rages and mourns about what happened to his father.

"She tried to apologize to us during the trial," Russel Towery said. " I got up and walked out. I'm sure other families are going through the same things I'm going through. It's been almost 19 years ... people forget."

"I don't want to die before she does. I want to stand there as she's kicking and screaming going to the death gurney. I want her to think about what my dad went through when she didn't even know his name," he said. "She thinks that because she said she was sorry, that everything's all right. ... she is evil and needs to be destroyed."

HUSBAND KILLER : THE TRUE STORY OF TRACEY GRISSOM

Claiming to be a victim of rape and other abuses, a distraught Tracey Grissom would travel to her ex-husband Hunter's workplace and shoot him six times in the back, receiving a twenty-five-year life sentence for his murder.

Her defense attorney would argue that Tracey was motivated by post-traumatic stress disorder caused by her Hunter's constant abuse and sexual assaults. One jury member had even asked the judge to be lenient in her sentencing as they were not allowed to hear details of her Hunter's alleged abuses (beatings, rape, sodomy).

But what really happened in the years that led up to May 15th, 2012? Was she in fact the victim of years of abuse by a psychotic husband? Or did she want to cash in on his $100,000 life insurance policy?

INSTANT ATTRACTION

The couple would meet during a dinner party in 2003 in Tuscaloosa, Alabama. Tracey was twenty-one years old and going through a divorce. She had a son, James Michael, from the previous marriage.

Family and friends would describe the union as "love at first sight." Hunter was blown away by the young Tracey's blue eyes and facial beauty.

"For him, it was love at first sight," crime author William Phelps said. "She was gorgeous."

A whirlwind courtship would ensue and the couple would elope in 2004.

"In the beginning, it was good," Tracey told CBS' 48 hours. "We had a friendship. Just your normal, honeymoon phase marriage."

"He was fun," Tracey said. "And he was attractive."

Hunter was two years younger than Tracey, however, and his mother felt that he had jumped the gun too early in the relationship.

Her words proved to be prophetic as after only eight months into the marriage, the marriage went south.

According to Tracey, their marital problems began with Hunter's drug addiction.

"I had caught him smoking marijuana," Tracey said. "Doing illegal things could cause a problem and I couldn't risk losing my son over."

Tracey claimed that she threatened her new spouse with a divorce but Hunter gave her his word that he would stop with his drug use. She stated that the relationship improved and the decided to start a construction company together.

"I took out an equity line to start a company," Tracey said. "Which was Grissom Construction. It was all in my name."

Hunter specialized in building elaborate boat docks. He had an artistic eye and could do docks, stairs, and other accouterments. The business began to grow in short order.

"They're going to take on the world," Phelps said. "They're going to be entrepreneurs and they're gonna make it."

They then had a daughter of their own, Anna Grace. The child was a long time coming for the couple. They had been trying for a long time as Tracey had five miscarriages before Anna Grace was born.

"She was premature," Tracey recalled. "Her heart and lungs were not developed. A very stressful time."

Behind closed doors things were rocky. On the surface, however, things looked good. They had a young family and were making money.

"All-American family," Phelps said. "White-picket fence. The whole nine yards. Middle-class. Suburbia. Maybe the Prince Charming that she's been waiting for."

But again, this was only on the surface. Tracey harbored secrets of her own. One of which was her own addiction to prescription drugs.

"Psychologically, there's something going on here," Phelps said. "There's something going on behind those beautiful eyes and it ain't good."

Tracey would often turn on on the children, showing off her temper. Then she would turn on Hunter.

"This would cause friction in the marriage," Phelps said. "And where there's friction, there's fire."

SETTING THE STAGE

Tracey would later state that Hunter would "act strangely" shortly before she filed divorce. She was a registered nurse and gave him an over-the-counter drug test. According to her, Hunter tested posted for marijuana, Oxycontin, opiates, and methamphetamine.

Hunter would later be arrested for marijuana possession but his family would insist that he never did the harder drugs.

Tracey would file for divorce in the summer of 2010 after six years of marriage. According to her, this would prompt physical abuse from Hunter.

Hunter had to move out but their divorce agreement would allow him access to the home.

"In September of 2010," Tracey recalled. "That was the first time he physically hit me. It (the abuse) got progressively worse. He had made the comments that if I told anybody he would kill me. I believed him."

Hunter' co-workers and family members would have a different take on the situation, however. His co-workers remembered a time when she tracked him down at one of the jobs and made a scene.

"She's screaming, jumping on him," Hunter's co-worker said. "Said something about him having another girlfriend and used the expression about, 'You are mine. I'll kill you. I'll kill you. You are mine."

"She's borderline demonic," Hunter's mother said. " mean, I absolutely believe—that she is that troubled."

Hunter's family continued to believe that he did not abuse Tracey.

"He did not have an abusive, an angry bone in his body," Hunter's aunt Gina said. "In fact, we kind of laughed at him because he was too laid-back."

The divorce was finalized in October of 2010.

EVIDENCE OF ABUSE?

Loran Richards was the first of Tracey's friends to notice the minor injuries on her body. She would inquire about the bruises but the answers she received were always evasive. Seeing Tracey with a black eye, however, forced her to try and get more answers.

"I said, Tracey, you may have terrible luck," Richards recalled. "But nobody is so unlucky that they trip, fall down the stairs, and hit their face on a baseball in the eye socket. So don't give me a lame excuse. You don't have to give me any excuse, but let's take a picture."

Tracey broke down. She gave her friend all of the grisly details, detailing the abuse she suffered at the hands of Hunter. Loran then became her advocate, taking pictures of Tracey's injuries. She would later state that she saw blood stains and other signs of abuse at Tracey's home.

THAT FATEFUL NIGHT

Now divorced, Hunter would arrive at Tracey's home on November 22nd, 2010.

According to Tracey, he then became enraged when Tracey told him that she had spent the night with a new lover.

"He told me that he was gonna kill me," Tracey recalled. Tracey stated that she tried to escape, running into the closet in order to "get away from the kids and to pray." Tracey's eleven-year-old son from a previous relationship was in the home as was the four-year-old daughter they have together.

Hunter caught up with her and knocked her to the ground. He tied a belt around her ankles and then began choking her.

Half-conscious, Tracey alleged to have been raped and sodomized.

The brutal attack would leave Tracey unconscious. She would wake up the next morning on the bathroom floor.

"I called Hunter," Tracey recalled. "I told him that I was bleeding and that I was hurt and that I needed help. And he told me, 'Fuck you. I hope you die."

Tracey wound up in the emergency room after the attack. Hospital records would show that she had a laceration on her head, bruises, and ligature marks on her feet.

Tracey would then be referred to the Turning Point domestic violence center.

Marian Waters would describe Tracey's injuries as among the worst she had ever seen in a twenty-year career.

Waters would testify that Tracey had suffered a horrific assault. She described her mental state as typical of someone who had just been raped; fearful, jumpy, fearing for her life.

Tracey had suffered a hematoma on her side that was the side of a grapefruit. She also claimed to have experienced rectal nerve damage which would require surgery as well as torn vaginal muscles requiring her to have a hysterectomy.

Police were called and Hunter would be arrested for rape, sodomy, kidnapping and domestic violence.

"And at that point, I feared for my life," Tracey recalled. "And I feared for my children's life."

A HIDDEN AGENDA

Hunter would be freed on bail but Tracey got a restraining order against him. She bought a gun and did not go anywhere unarmed.

She took photos of her injuries on the night of the alleged attack and texted them to Loran. Later, they would take more pictures.

Angered, Hunter would stop paying her spousal and child support. Tracey, however, may have had another scenario in mind for obtaining money.

She had forced Hunter to take out a $103,000 life insurance policy around the time their daughter was born.

On May 24, 2012, the day before Tracey shot Hunter, she would place a call to MetLife that was recorded.

"Thank you for calling MetLife, this is Pam. May I please have your name?"

"Tracey Grissom."

Tracey would then explain that she was angry that her husband stopped making payments on his policy. During their divorce proceedings, he had agreed to continue paying the premiums. Tracey stated she was calling to make sure that they had the correct address on file.

"Is there anything else I can do for you today?

"That's gonna be it!" Tracey said, hanging up.

"Well, May 14th was just like any other day," Tracey said, explaining the call to the insurance company. "However, I had moved four different times. Me and my children were running. We were running from Hunter. So I had called the company to let them know that they had my old address and to make an address change."

FALSE RAPE?

Shelly Standridge was hired by Hunter to defend him in the rape case. She would state that Hunter denied raping or even assaulting Tracey that night. Hunter did, however, admit to the fact that he and his wife had consensual sex that night...Rough consensual sex.

"So that night," Standridge said. "Hunter said that she was depressed and claiming she was going to kill herself. She was saying she wanted their relationship to work."

So she undressed in front of him. Her beauty was always impossible for Hunter to resist.

The two had sex despite Hunter having a new girlfriend at home.

Hunter's aunt, Gina, believed that Tracey wanted to kill Hunter before the rape case went to court.

"He had a new girlfriend, he was living with her," Phelps said. "He was moving on with his life. Hunter would claim that Tracey was jealous, obsessive, even stalked them."

"Hunter had moved on," Hunter's aunt said. "There was some court dates coming up that would prove that Hunter was innocent. There were court dates coming up that he would get visitation to his daughter. She had a lot to lose."

Tracey was on the anti-anxiety drug Klonopin. Hunter would tell his attorney that Tracey would take more than her prescribed dose. Because of this, she fell and cut her head. Hunter would then leave the house around 10:30 pm and go to his father's house. Tracey would call him hours later, at 3:20 am.

Hunter would state that Tracey had called to threaten him. She told him if he didn't want the responsibility of the children then she would make it where he would never be able to see them again.

Hunter's attorney did not know what Tracey's motive was for crying rape. She was very upset that he had a girlfriend.

MORE LIES...

Hunter would be arrested nearly twelve hours later, to his total shock.

Tracey would give her side of the story to the police which later is proven to be false.

She would tell police that Hunter had thrown her against the bathtub around 10 pm and claim to be unconscious until 4 am the next morning.

"But her phone records show she was on the phone all night, so she was never unconscious," Standridge said. "She was also using her data at 10:42 that night. She was using it again at 10:50 that night. ... She sends a text to her boyfriend at 1:49 am. She sends a text to her friend at 2:07 am. She sends another text to her boyfriend at 2:07 am."

Tracey would blame the calls on Hunter.

"All I do know is I was not the only person using my phone that night," Tracey said, suggesting that Hunter used her phone.

Medical records would show that Tracey's head wound was "purely superficial".

Only one suture was needed.

Furthermore, there was nothing on the medical record to support the fact that Tracey experienced vaginal and rectal tears. She did have bruises on her ankle and legs but the photos taken by police at the emergency room would not resemble the same photos that Tracey and her friend Loran would take days later. In the photos taken at the emergency room, an area of Tracey's body has no bruises. Days later, there is discoloration.

Tracey's attorney would blame the discrepancy on "blood thinners" which would cause Tracey to bruise easily.

There was also a discrepancy in her phone records. She would take a photo of her inner thigh, a deep bruise. This area of her body was not photographed by police during her emergency room visit. But on December 9th, almost two weeks later, Tracey took a photo of her inner thigh with the deep bruise

"He (Hunter) told me that he would make it to where nobody would ever want me," Tracey said after a 2010 attack. "I didn't report it because I thought he would kill me."

THE FINAL STRAW

Tracey woke up pissed on May 15th, 2012.

Hunter had been ordered to pay $2,100 a month for the rest of his life. He was not complying with the court order claiming that he was "out of work."

Tracey stated that she was on her way to a job interview when she saw a Grissom Construction sign out of the corner of her eye.

She stated that her initial plan was to take a photograph of Hunter at the job site in order to show proof that he was working as part of her litigation.

"I was getting ready to take the picture and when I looked up he was standing almost directly towards the front of the boat trailer," Tracey said. "He was looking back directly at me. He had this face, that's like mean - just, I don't know how to describe it. I mean, I see it over and over like it's right there all the time. He flipped me the bird, which to me was kinda like, 'Yeah I'm workin. Screw you.' And at that point, I panicked. At that point, I didn't know what else to do except to defend myself."

Tracey started firing. The first shot hit Hunter in the arm. He started to run and she fired again repeatedly. One of the bullets punctured Hunter's heart and he died of massive internal bleeding.

William Dockery was working with Hunter and was an eyewitness to the shooting. Hunter had turned to Dockery before the shooting and told him to "call the law". Before Dockery could pick up his cell phone, Tracey had commenced shooting.

Tracey then pulled out her own cell phone and called the cops on herself. She tearfully described that she had just murdered her husband.

CONFESSION

Tracey told detectives exactly what was going through her mind when she came upon Hunter at the construction site.

"Tell me about what happened," the detective said. "What led up to...what's going on."

"In November of 2010, he beat me unconscious and raped me...and, and left me for dead....and, and I finally pressed charges against him and he told me that he would make my life a living hell...and that's what he's done."

"What, what happened this morning that led up to you going..."

"I was going to work and I saw him...and he's been claiming that he-he's not working. And, so I pulled in there to take a picture of him...cause it was the truck that's still in my name...and the boat that's still in my name...and the trailer that's still in my name...He just stared at me and flipped me off...and I just went in there and shot him...I just shot him, I shot him, and I shot him."

Tracey would be distraught and tearful during her interrogation room confession. A few weeks later, however, she would call the insurance company to let them know that Hunter had died.

"Well, I was actually calling because I didn't know what I needed to do ... Hunter passed away May 15th and I actually am going a court case right now because it was due to self-defense..."

Hunter's family went ballistic over this. Tracey would claim that she had no money but she continued to pay his life insurance premiums.

"Even through the times when she's screamin' that she's destitute and has no money ... she continued to pay life insurance premium," Hunter's mother said.

"I don't think my sister concocted a story," Tracey's sister said. "Just so she could get insurance money. ... But that's all they (the prosecution) had."

THE TRIAL

Tracey's allegations of rape and sodomy would not be allowed in court testimony. She was allowed, however, to detail the effects of Hunter's abuse on her were.

Taking the stand, Tracey would lift up her shirt in court and show herself wearing a colostomy bag. She stated that she had undergone several surgeries after her husband's daily rapes wherein she suffered permanent rectal and vaginal damage.

Hunter's family was then allowed to speak at the hearing.

"This tremendous loss has changed me," Hunter's mother, Melanie Garner said. "And I don't know how to change back."

Chloe, Hunter's sister, had a victim's services officer read her letter in court.

"Tracey is psychotic," Chloe wrote. "She is the most selfish person human being on this earth."

"Every mother should pray every night that your son doesn't fall in love with someone like Tracey," Hunter's aunt, Gina Grissom said. "There have been lots of allegations against Hunter. We've never believed anything that has come out of her (Tracey's) mouth."

His aunt then looked directly at Tracey.

"Hunter was proud of his name. Why would you still choose to use our name, and bring it down?" suggesting that if Tracey hated him so much why didn't she go revert to her maiden name after the divorce.

The jurors would find Tracey guilty of murder. She would be sentenced to twenty-five years in prison.

One of the jurors, Janice Kelly, would contact Grissom's attorney Warren Freeman the morning after the trial. She had remorse over her decision and said that she wouldn't have convicted her had they had the rapes and abuse allegations been introduced as evidence.

"I feel I made a mistake," Kelly said. "If I had to do it over again, we'd have had a hung jury. We didn't get her side. She did not get a fair trial."

"We voted to convict because there was no dispute that Tracey shot Hunter," the jury foreman wrote in a letter that was addressed in the courthouse. "Jurors didn't believe prosecutor claims that she did it in order to collect a life insurance policy. We felt the shooting was a crime of passion, not for financial gain and that she should be sentenced accordingly. I wish we had seen evidence of the rape allegation. We feel that she just 'lost it.'"

"It's not fair, it's not fair!" Tracey sobbed as she was led out of the courthouse and to jail.

"We think the sentencing was too harsh," Tracey's attorney Warren Freeman said. "Considering you have the foreperson of the jury actually saying, we don't feel like she should be punished according to being found guilty of murder. Let's just say that there will be a basis for a new trial, and part of it will be something that the jurors saw that they weren't supposed to see and I'm going to just leave it at that until I file my motion."

"My son died running for his life," Hunter's mother said. "I don't know what was running through his mind but I hear him say 'momma.'"

"People who think that I murdered him in cold blood," Tracey said. "Either don't know the whole story or don't know everything that's happened.

Tracey was asked on CBS' 48 hours if she regretted pulling the trigger on that fateful day.

"No," she said flatly. "Because if I hadn't I would be dead. I truly believe that."

"She has a way of making everything she does look right," Hunter's aunt, Gina scoffed.

GOD TOLD ME TO: THE TRUE STORY OF GWEN HENDRICKS

85

Gwen Gillespie Hendricks was born into a Navy family in Memphis, Tennessee in 1955.

Her father was a naval officer while her mother was a housewife. Like most military families, they moved often from station to station, according to her father's assignment. Growing up in a devoutly Catholic home and Gwen would embrace the religion with fervor.

Gwen dressed with modesty, wearing button down shirts and minimal make-up. She fostered a nerd look, with wire-rimmed glasses and short hair.

Carrying on the family's military tradition, she joined the Air Force at the age of twenty-five. It was there she would meet Jim Hendricks, twenty-four, who was her instructor.

Jim Hendricks was a tall, strapping Air Force sergeant with an air of authority. He had an easy smile and Gwen found him easy on the eyes.

"Well, it was kind of instant attraction," Gwen recalled. "There was a bit of lust there as he's a very tall, handsome man. The Air Force can tell you that you can't date but they can't tell you who to marry so I went to the Jag office and asked if I could marry my STA and they said 'yes.'"

The two were married in 1980. Jim had a five year old daughter, Season Hendricks, from a previous relationship. In 1982, they would have a son, Ben.

Because of their career choice, the couple spent a lot of time apart during the early years of their marriage. Jim was stationed at Wake Island while Gwen was assigned to Eglin Air Force Base in Florida.

The couple would be reunited in 1986 as Jim was assigned to the Air Force Academy in Colorado Springs. Gwen would not re-enlist in the Air Force, instead taking a job with the Internal Revenue Service.

The couple spent three years in Colorado before Jim would be transferred to Guam in August of 1989. He took the the entire family with him to the island.

"I figured we had a pretty normal family," Season said. "Until we moved to Guam. Things started to change. She (Gwen) would pick fights. She was jealous of the time my Dad and I would spend together."

"She (Gwen) had a different life in mind for herself," forensic psychologist Joyce Smith said. "She was used to having her own money. So when they moved to Guam there was little to do and less money to do it with."

Gwen and the children moved back to the United States, returning to Colorado and leaving Jim in Guam.

She would buy a home in Littleton and once again start working for the IRS. She then joined the junior Chamber of Commerce where she met Terry Knaack and a woman named Rochelle.

"Rochelle was into tarot cards," Gwen said. "And Terry was into new age occultism. My religion, my faith was still very meaningful to me. I wanted to do Bible study with them to get them out of what I considered witchcraft. Rochelle said she wouldn't go to Bible study with me unless I did the cards with her and the same with Terry. So I think I opened up the door to hell. Right after I started, everything went wrong"

During this time, Gwen began to experience health issues. She suffered from dizzy spells and nausea.

Her personality shifted as well, changing from being even-tempered to easily agitated and manic. With her health and ability to focus effected, Gwen stepped down from her revenue collector position to tax examiner.

"Could the illness have played a part in her deciding to kill her husband?" Smith asked. "Maybe. But Gwen was really steeped into religion and sounded like she embraced some of the more fringe elements of Christianity. She truly believed that occultism was a form of witchcraft and that those things could do her harm. So when she suffered from her illness she erroneously attributed it to her dabbling in the occult. She was a woman who preferred supernatural explanations to rational thought."

Gwen also started to grow deeper into debt, buying expensive gifts for friends.

In the fall of 1990, Gwen hired Terry Knaack to help remodel the Littleton home. A few months later, Knaack moved into the couple's basement with the rationale being he would be able to help with the mortgage. With the husband away and a man in the home, Gwen began to fantasize about Terry and starting over with him.

"Terry would talk a lot about wanting to having a ranch for children with special needs," Gwen recalled. "And I started having delusions that he and I would start this ranch together for the children."

"She entered into a fantasy world," Smith said. "She began imagining a life with this other man, having delusions of grandeur of what they would do together. He became her willing accomplice in her dreams, since her own husband was absent because of military duty. So an alternate universe with Terry Knaack became her obsession. What probably started as harmless day dreams soon grew into something sinister."

"I also believe that Gwen had more than a little bit of a Messiah complex. She had this compulsion to save people and it manifested in doling out gifts and handouts to people who she felt were in need. She had this secret life and kept things from Jim who was away on military assignment. Those secrets involved getting into credit card debt."

By January of 1991, Gwen began telling friends that she was having premonitions of Jim dying in a plane crash.

"I had this really bad dream over and over again," Gwen recalled. "Where Jim had died in a plane crash. I was thinking, well after Jim died that I would marry Terry and we'd start this ranch but of course Terry didn't know anything about because it was all in my head."

Gwen then began hearing voices.

"They (the voices) wanted me to sacrifice what was most dear in my life," Gwen recalled. "I remember thinking that I have to answer these voices because this is coming from God. You know, I've got to sacrifice what I loved the most and that was Jim."

Gwen kept a journal where she logged the "premonitions" of her husband's death. She titled the journal "The Courage to Will and Persevere," She described the voices that she heard and believed that God had told her to kill Jim.

"She experienced what we call 'command hallucinations,'" said Smith. "These are sometimes coupled with someone's value system, in this case, it was Gwen's religion. Gwen believed that she should obey God and believed that the voices that she heard were, in fact, coming from God. So this could go bad real quick if those voices told her to do damage to someone."

"She was past the breaking point, a delusional schizophrenic that was not diagnosed. When she confided with friends it was probably with people who shared her same point of view, people who believed in visions, messages from God and premonitions. Gwen was a soft-spoken woman and even if someone thought she was crazy they would not think she would be capable of taking a gun and blowing someone's brains out. She didn't have that violent vibe."

But behind closed doors, Gwen would deal with problems or difficulties in a haphazard fashion. She would often open up the Bible and believed that whatever random verse she came upon was a direct message from God.

"I reread Psalm 90 quite a few times before a small voice said, 'Keep reading, keep reading.'" Gwen wrote in her journal. "After reading the first page of stanzas, I knew I would be protected from the car bombs, the knifings, the guns, the contracts and all the other evil I had seen connected with busting the pornographers and pimps. Those mafia guys play rough, but somehow they just won't be able to get me. Then I turned the page to continue reading. It felt like a giant fist had slammed into my heart. I literally could not breath [sic]. I burst into sobs and sunk to the floor. I cried for Jim because he really was going to die."

Gwen began to prepare for Jim's death, taking out a $300,000 life insurance policy on her husband payable on his death.

She then visited a local banker, informing him that she would be soon be receiving proceeds from insurance claim. Gwen was told that she would not be able to use the money as long as Jim was alive. She then forged a doctor's note which alleged that she had multiple sclerosis. She submitted this note to the Red Cross along with a letter stating that they should be responsible for being her husband back from Guam.

Gwen did not want the proceeds from the insurance for her own material gain. She believed that she could use the proceeds from his life insurance to establish the "James Hendricks Foundation" to aid victims of mafia produced pornography.

"She became obsessed with pornographers," Smith said. "Like most people with Messiah Complexes, she chose an ill of society and focused on that, believing that she was a chosen vessel to help eradicate the 'sin'. In her deluded mind, she needed this money to accommodate

God's will to establish this ranch wherein she would save victims of pornography. The only way she could attain this goal would be to kill Jim and take the life insurance proceeds."

"I was very desperate to have him (Jim) back," Gwen said. "I felt like I was at my limit and not really realizing that I actually was really having a breakdown."

With her husband not even dead yet, Gwen began purchasing clothes for herself and the children to wear for his funeral.

She bought silk flowers and boxes of Kleenex for mourning friends and family.

Gwen also increased the amount of Jim's life insurance from $300,000 to $1,000,000.

True to her premonition, she bought a wedding dress for herself and put a wedding ring on layaway for Knaack.

Gwen would ask God to speak to her directly and "guide her hand" as she thumbed through her Bible. When she got to a passage, she would believe that was what God wanted her to study."

"For the first reading, only the last sentence made sense," Gwen wrote. *"I had asked if what I felt about Jim's death was real. He said yes.*

God can even speak through the dictionary!

After reading the first page of stanzas, I knew I would be protected from car bombs, the knifings, the guns, the contracts and all the other evil I had seen connected with busting pornographers and pimps. Those Mafia guys play rough, but somehow they just won't be able to get me."

"You can see her delusions of grandeur in her journal writings," Smith said. "She had all of the symptoms of a delusional narcissist, truly believing that God made her as the 'Chosen One.'"

Gwen would write that she had a two-way conversation with God about creating the ranch.

"Oh, so the ranch is in Douglas county near to the Springs so my family will be protected from the mafia guys' Then I knew in Denver, I'm Gwen Hendricks. In the Springs, I'm Gwen Knaack. I had thought the clinic would carry the name of the ranch, but with this new insight, I knew that for safety sake, everything had to be kept separate."

She continued to have health issues as well, as the nausea and attacks of dizziness still had not subsided. Physicians could not determine the cause of her illness. She was eventually diagnosed with Ménière's disease, an ailment that causes vertigo and a fluctuating hearing loss. She had a micro-shunt placed into her ear which only helped relieve the pain she was experiencing.

Her mental health, however, continued to deteriorate.

Jim would return to Colorado for good in May of 1991. It would not be a well-received reunion, however, as the couple fought over everything specifically the living arrangements of Knaack. Jim promptly kicked the boarder out of the home.

He then took control of the finances as he discovered that Gwen had maxed out the credit cards.

"My brother said that she had apparently taken several other credit cards and had maxed them out to the limit," recalled Steve Hendricks, Jim's brother. "And he was furious with her at that point. He did confide in me that he was thinking about leaving Gwen."

Jim would take away all of Gwen's credit cards and this made her extremely angry.

"He took away her power," Smith said. "She got an ego boost by buying expensive gifts for friends and helping out women that she thought were in need. When Jim took that away, she saw him as someone who needed to be eliminated."

Divorce seemed imminent but Gwen seemed immune to it all in her journal writings.

"The funeral, the ranch school, children, the foundation, always being pushed forward," she wrote. "I have to do what I have to do, too. But just for now I'm going to take one day at a time. I'm hoping I don't get too compulsed to do anything more for at least this coming week. I need to rest.

Perhaps I should start by explaining the little voice. It's my voice, but not me. It comes from somewhere inside, and if I don't listen to it, act on it, it becomes a compulsion. If I don't listen and act on the compulsion, it grows stronger and stronger until it dominates all aspects of my life. I learned long ago to listen and do what I'm told. Things work out when I do, and when I don't, things get real miserable...Yes, my little voice is the way God reaches me with the Holy Spirit."

With Jim now home on a permanent basis, The voices in her head grew louder. They began to speak with more urgency in telling her that she had to kill her husband.

"True to her religious background, she did not interpret auditory hallucinations as a sign of mental illness," Smith said. "Gwen was the kind of woman who took the stories in the Bible literally, seeing herself as a modern day Abraham who heard voices from God. You hear it in the way she describes the voices in her head telling her to sacrifice her husband in the same way the Bible speaks of God telling Abraham to sacrifice his son Isaac."

"I said 'Lord I surrender to you,'" Gwen recalled. "I'm hearing voices from God and this is what God wants and I have to get this from God and if this is what God wants then I have to give it to him. So I went out and I bought a gun"

"The voices in her head told her it was time," Smith said. "And true to her value system, she had to obey. For her religion was not a therapeutic aid because of the way she had viewed it. Her God was a vengeful one, a violent one."

On Friday, August 17th, 1991 Gwen drove to Peterson Air Force Base to meet with her husband, a 75 mile drive, to bring him a change of clothes.

"Jim was working late and he asked me to bring him something to eat." Gwen said.

She had informed police that Jim was working all night to prepare for an inspection but changed his mind.

Gwen wrote in her journal about the incident.

When Jim called to say he was on his way home, I went into shock. I knew the time was at hand. I knew I wasn't really ready. I screamed and cried and raged. Then I asked again, if he was meant to die or was I just suckered into some kind of head game. Benjamin's daddy died. I cried myself to sleep that night. I thought what was I supposed to do with two husbands. God has the oddest sense of humor."

"She told me that she was gonna make a nice little picnic for them," Gwen's step-daughter Season recalled. "They were going to make a night of it and that she wanted him to feel good for his inspection."

Gwen left the home and dropped off both Season and son Ben with a friend. When Gwen arrived at the Air Force base, however, she stated that Jim told her that he was heading home. She maintained that the two then went back home in separate cars.

"His truck was in the lead," Gwen said. "I was in the car behind. I remember being so tired, I told him I can't go on anymore. I just want a quick nap and let's get in the back of the truck."

She said that they traveled in separate cars but she became tired and slept through the night at a rest stop along Interstate 25.

Police, however, believed that Gwen lured Jim to an abandoned stretch of highway with the promise of sex.

The two met at the side of the road and Gwen hesitated when thinking of pulling out the gun. She wanted her husband to go peacefully.

"I took the gun out from underneath the seat of the car," Gwen said. "I got into the truck and laid next to him and when I could feel that he was deeply sleeping that's when I shot him."

Gwen would shoot Jim six times.

"It was like I was outside of myself," Gwen said. "Looking and watching what I was doing. I felt very numb, very cold, like I was on auto-pilot. I got back into my car and I took apart the gun and I was just throwing the parts out the window and just driving around, just in a fog, not knowing what I was doing, where I was going. I stopped at a roadside rest stop. Fell asleep. When I woke up and I didn't know everything that happened."

When Gwen arrived back home that Saturday she began making calls to the police, stating that her husband was missing.

On Monday morning, she called Jim's supervisor who sent out two officers to search for him.

One of his co-workers would find his pickup truck on the side of Highway 83 in Douglas County. His body had been placed in the camper shell in back of his truck.

He had been shot six times in the chest and neck with a small caliber handgun.

Gwen would become the primary suspect.

Police noted that she hardly showed any emotion when they informed her of her husband's death.

"Her state of mind was that of a wife with a missing husband," one of the deputies recalled. "When she was telling a story, she couldn't stick with the same story. And that's a clue, obviously, to law enforcement."

Gwen would then break the news to Jim's daughter, Season.

"Gwen said they found him by the side of the road in his car," Season said. "And that he had been murdered. I don't remember her crying. It was the worst moment of my life."

Terry Knaack would be helpful in the case against Gwen. She had been secretly in love with him and given him her diary. He read through her writings and promptly delivered the diary to the Douglas County Sheriff's Department. The sheriffs then instructed him to call Gwen while they would listen in.

Gwen would tell Knaack that she didn't kill Jim but that she wanted to die. Then Douglas County Sheriff's Department Kim Castellano's intuition told her something was wrong. The Hendricks had two pre-teens, a boy and a girl and the boy was never around during questioning.

Castellano believed that Gwen had a problem with males. With one of the male investigators, an Air Force official, by her side, Castellano went back to talk to Gwen.

Once again, the boy was not there. Gwen was overly polite to Castellano, asking her if she wanted anything to eat and jumping up to fix her something before she could answer.

Gwen would totally ignored the male detective.

Castellano used this knowledge to her advantage and befriended Gwen, sensing that the delusional woman would be much more forthcoming with a female officer than a male.

Gwen began trusting her enough that she asked for Castellano's help in balancing her check book. The detective then saw that Hendricks had recently taken out several insurance policies that would be hers when her husband died.

The investigators then used a technique police refer to as the "midnight confession." Castellano and the Air Force official went over to the Hendricks house at eleven at night, waking Gwen up.

Questioning her in the family room, Gwen continued to deny her involvement in her husband's killing. Castellano and her partner then took turns reading from Gwen's journal, tightening the screws on her denial. They also saw Jim's watch on the counter.

Castellano then told her to get dressed and that she was being taken in.

Gwen finally cracked. She curled into a fetal position and confessed.

"Two stories that night—the story of the rest area and the story of Highway 83," she sobbed.

Gwen would go on to describe the highway story.

"There is blood everywhere, I can see it everywhere," she said. "It's terrible. My mind won't let me remember. I don't know if I shot him or not. I don't know what's real anymore."

Gwen was then taken to a local hospital where she stayed for two days for a mental health evaluation. She was arrested upon release and charged with her husband's murder.

After undergoing another mental health examination, Gwen was deemed delusional but understood the charges being levied against her.

Because of this, she was found fit to stand trial.

In court, however, Gwen continued to state that she didn't kill her husband. She said that the body found at the crime scene was not Jim's.

"There was the obvious choice for her attorneys to declare her insane," Smith said. "She had one hell of an imagination and could make things up on the fly. She said during the trial that she became completely convinced that her husband was still alive, going into full blown denial. 'He's still alive, he's out there somewhere and you have to find him', she would say. She was completely delusional."

Her first attorney, Lloyd Boyer, stated that it was physically impossible for Gwen to have murdered Jim Hendricks.

"The lack of gunshot residue inside the Capitol (Jim's car) vehicle," Boyer said. "Indicated that the murder had not occurred in the vehicle. Mr. Hendricks was quite a bit larger than Gwen and she was small, not especially strong and could not have moved the victim into the vehicle."

The investigators failed to produce the gun that Gwen used but the prosecution had another tool at its disposal.

The first link was Jim's watch that they found in Gwen's possession, which showed that she had tampered with the crime scene. The prosecution showed how she was going to use the money from the insurance policies and start a "home for troubled people" that would be near the spot where she killed her husband.

The jury found her guilty of first-degree murder and Hendricks was sentenced to life in prison.

"I just kept my faith that Jim would come rescue me and I would be set free from prison," Gwen said. "Of course, that never happened."

Inside the prison, physicians deemed her to be mentally unfit to be included with the general population and transferred her to the psychiatric unit.

"They got me on anti-psychotics," Gwen said. "And anti-depressants but it wasn't until 1997 that I started having memories of what had happened. At first, it was like just pictures and they hit me like bricks, you know. I killed a great husband and Dad. I robbed Season and Ben of their father. I felt lower than dirt."

She did have help, however, as some legal advocates filed briefs on her behalf, claiming that she had been insane at the time of her trial.

In September of 2000, the Supreme Court of Colorado overturned Gwen's conviction and ordered a new trial.

In April of 2001, a judge ruled that Gwen was not guilty by reason of insanity.

The trial lasted ten minutes.

"She came to terms with what she had done," Smith said. "She had stopped protesting, stop denying and admitted to what she had done."

Gwen was then remanded to a psychiatric care facility in Colorado. She then decided to change her name to "Emi Masai".

"When I lost Jim," Gwen said. "I also lost my children. I longed to be a wife and mother again. I redefined myself as married to Christ and being a mother to all the people I meet."

"By renaming herself she thought that she could obtain a new identity," Smith said. "It was a way of divorcing herself from her past transgressions."

Gwen went through four years of psychiatric treatment where the physicians determined that she was no longer a threat to society. She was released to a residential program where she now helps the needy at Mercy Ministries.

She continues to take her anti-psychotic medication.

"I never want to slip back into mental illness again," Gwen said. "I literally thank God every morning I open my medicine cabinet. I've always said justice wasn't done. Justice in this case would have been my execution. A life for a life. But it's not about fairness. It's about recognizing mental illness and knowing that you're not responsible for what you are doing when you're psychotic."

Gwen has had minimal contact with both her son and step-daughter since she committed the murder of their father.

"I long to see them but they let it be known through family channels that they don't want to see me," Gwen said. "So I respect that."

"I'm really glad that Gwen has helped herself enough to admit what she's done," Season said. "And I hope there never is a time where it gets easy for her to look in the mirror. Because there's never a time where it's easy to be without our Dad."

"I wish I could take it back," Gwen said. "Be a good wife and Mom again. I can't turn the clock back. So all I can do is give them my deepest apology and ask them to forgive me."

BURY THEM ALIVE : THE TRUE STORY OF SERIAL KILLER TIFFANY COLE

JESSICA WINSTON

When James "Reggie" and Carol Sumner moved to Jacksonville, Florida for their retirement, they had visions of good health and happiness. They never thought that their overnight invitation to long-time South Carolina neighbor, Tiffany Cole, would end up the way it did; With the Sumner couple being buried alive.

Reggie and Carol Sumner were high school sweethearts in North Charleston, South Carolina. They were the kind of couple that everyone envied as they walked down the hall. Unfortunately, their lives pulled them in different directions. Reggie decided to serve his country in the navy. After finishing his tour, he got married and landed a job with the railroad. Carol also married and became a devoted mother, however, her first marriage ended in divorce, and her second nearly killed her. In 1987, after years of abuse, her husband at the time shot her seven times in their home before driving away and turning the gun on himself. Her daughter, Rhonda Alford, just ten years old at that time, spent almost a year helping her mother recover from her wounds. She had to help her bathe, dress, and take care of the house. After taking eight years to fully recover, Carol went back to work as soon as she was able. For over twenty-five years she was a civil servant at the Citadel and the Charleston Air Force Base. She also worked a second job at night at a Belk department store, among other jobs she would take when needed. She did whatever she had to in order to make ends meet. Shortly after her recovery, she found out that the blood transfusion she had received during her previous trauma had given her Hepatitis C. She was angry because she felt as though she could not escape her late ex-husband, but she refused to let it ruin her life. She soon started a new job at a cable company and it was during this time that her life finally changed for the better. Nearly forty years after they'd left high school, a chance encounter brought Carol and Reggie together again. One night in 2000, a phone call was made to the cable company where Carol was working, which she received. After talking with the customer Carol and learning his name, she realized that he also sounded just like the Reggie she remembered. So she asked him if he was the same Reggie Sumner who attended Garrett High school in South Charleston. It was. They decided that they should get together after not seeing each other in so long. This time, though they were inseparable. Like "teenagers in love", a quick courtship led to love and then marriage in 2001 with a ceremony at Carol's home in West Ashley. Carol's daughter has said of Reggie "he was just a very gentle, kind and giving spirit. You could not ask for a better friend, husband or stepfather." Eventually, after retiring, the couple decided to move from South Carolina to Jacksonville, Florida. Reggie had previously bought a house during his days working for CSX railroad and as he was a "brittle" diabetic in frail health, he thought he would be more comfortable in the warmer climate. Carol agreed. "She only went down there to honor her husband," Rhonda said. Before moving, they decided to sell their Chevrolet Lumina to the stepdaughter of a friend who lived down the street, Tiffany Cole. They allowed her to make payments on the car to help her out and she agreed, often driving down to Jacksonville with friends to make those payments. Tiffany and the Sumners became friends and Tiffany would often spend the night at their house when she and her friends went down south. A pleasant girl on the outside, the Sumners had no idea what Tiffany could really be like.

Tiffany Ann Cole was born on December 3, 1981, to her sixteen-year-old mother, Shirley Duncan. Her biological father was in jail. She had no male role model to look up to or who could offer her protection the way a father should. Her mother had a boyfriend, but he was beyond cruel and especially loved to torment Tiffany. At one point, she had a puppy which her stepdad threw against a wall, breaking its neck right in front of her. He was abusive verbally as well as physically and Tiffany claims that as a young girl, he began to molest her, beginning around age eight. As a young teenager, she turned to alcohol and drugs to deal with the pain. In high school, Tiffany was a student who participated in cheerleading and played the flute. She was also a girl scout member but eventually the alcohol and drugs took over her life and she quit her programs and dropped out of school. At one point she fell in love with a boy with severe epilepsy, who ended up breaking her heart and since the only example of love from a man came from an abusive stepfather, this breakup reinforced the belief that she should expect to be treated badly and let down by men. She began looking for love in all the wrong places. In May of 2005, during a six-month period of prostitution, Tiffany ran into a man by the name of Michael Jackson. They were drawn to each other right away and began to get high and sleep together.

Michael James Jackson, born May 12, 1982, had a significant criminal history beginning in childhood. Born to a drug-addicted mother, he was mostly raised by his grandmother. He had multiple felony convictions but only for things like fraud and theft. After meeting Tiffany and becoming close, they took a road trip, first going to Myrtle Beach, then driving to Jacksonville, Florida, where they would be staying with Michael's best friend, Alan Wade. Born May 22, 1987, Alan and Michael had known each other for just over a year. When Tiffany and Michael arrived in Florida, they stayed at Alan's mom's house. After just a few days, though, she kicked them out because she was tired of the loud noises and constant partying. With nowhere else to go and with all their money spent on the nights of drinking and partying, Tiffany remembered that the Sumners lived nearby. The three friends showed up at their doorstep and explained what had happened. The couple was very happy to see Tiffany and invited her and her friends to stay the night. While they were chatting and catching up, Carol mentioned how worried they had been about their house in North Carolina not selling. There was no need to worry, however, because not only did their property sell, but they had also made a $99,000 profit. It was this general statement to a long-time neighbor that sealed the Sumner's fate.

It's difficult to know just whose idea it was to rob the Sumner's. Some say it was both Tiffany and Michael, while others say it was Michael who was the plan maker and master manipulator. Either way, a plan was hatched to rob and kill the loving couple. At some point in June, Alan had contacted his friend, Bruce Nixon Jr., and told him of a plan to rob someone. No other details were given. Then on July 6th, Alan called Bruce, born May 9th, 1987, and asked him if he would be interested in joining the others in digging a hole. Bruce agreed and stole four shovels from his neighborhood. The other three friends drove to Bruce's house in a rented Mazda RX-8 that Tiffany had rented in South Carolina. The group drove around hoping to find a perfectly remote place for the hole to be dug. Alan asked Bruce if he knew of any good places to which Bruce responded that he did. He took them into Georgia, to a wooded area just over the state line. Leaving the car parked on the road, the group walked through the wooded area into a clearing where they began to dig a hole while Tiffany held a flashlight. It was approximately four feet deep and six feet square. Upon completion of the hole, they left the shovels and went back to the car. It was here that Alan asked Michael if Bruce could join in on their robbery plan. Michael agreed. The foursome drove back to Alan's house but his mother would not allow Michael in as she believed him to be a bad influence on her son. Over the next couple of days, it was

Tiffany's job to remain in contact with Carol and Reggie in order to gain information from them about their plans and whereabouts. The foursome also secretly watched the house in order to figure out the Sumner's routine. It was unclear yet as to whether or not the group would enter the home while the couple was gone or if they would simply go in with the couple there. It was ultimately decided that they would enter the home while the couple was there so that they could get their financial information and the means to access their accounts. Michael said that he would kill the victims by injecting them with a lethal dose of their medications. He then promised that the four friends would split the money they received from the Sumner's accounts, each receiving about $50,000. They began making preparations for their plan. Just after midnight on July 8th, 2005, Michael, Tiffany, and Alan went to Wal-Mart and purchased disposable rubber gloves. On the evening of the murders, they went to an Office Depot, where Tiffany bought duct tape and a large roll of plastic wrap. Last, they bought a toy gun that shot plastic pellets.

Around 10pm., on July 8th, 2005, Tiffany drove the other three group members to the Sumner's house in the Mazda. Herself and Michael remained in the car while Alan and Bruce went up to the door. They had the duct tape and toy gun and both were wearing the plastic gloves. After Carol answered the door, Bruce and Alan told her that they were having car trouble and asked if they could use their phone. Carol said of course they could and invited them in. As soon as the boys entered the home, Alan pulled the phone cord out of the wall. Bruce pointed the gun at the couple. Alan grabbed Reggie around the neck and pushed him down into a chair. They told the couple that they wanted credit and debit cards and any other financial information. Carol began pleading with the boys not to hurt them. Bruce took the couple into a spare bedroom where he used duct tape to bind their legs and hands and to cover their mouths and eyes. Alan sent a text message to Michael, informing him that everything was under control. Michael then also entered the home and he and Alan began searching for financial information. They saw a pile of mail and financial statements which they put into a plastic bag. They spotted Reggie's prized coin collection and took that too. Michael told the other two to take the couple into the garage at which point they put them into the trunk of the Lincoln Town car. Tiffany went into the house and grabbed some of their belongings, put them into a bag and took the bag with her to the Mazda. Following the plan, both cars headed towards the gravesite, stopping only once to put gas in the Lincoln. Upon arrival at the site, Michael opened the trunk and apparently began screaming when he saw that the duct tape had become loose and the couple had worked the tape off. It had been over 100 degrees in the trunk. Sweat had caused the tape to loosen. They had also taken the tape off their eyes and were huddled together. Michael ordered Bruce to tape them up again, which he did. Alan then attempted to back up the car to the edge of the grave but, unable to do so, Bruce took over. Michael then sent Bruce up the road to wait with Tiffany at the Mazda. While still alive, the Sumners were taken out of the trunk and pushed into the hole. It is unclear as to who actually did the burying because Alan and Michael each blamed the other. Somehow, Michael ended up getting the personal identification number of the Sumner's bank account. Reports differ on whether he obtained this information from somewhere in the house or if Carol told him the number while being threatened to be buried alive. According to one documentary, Carol had gotten the tape off her mouth again when in the hole. Michael was telling them that if they didn't give up their PIN, they would die, at which point Carol yelled it out. It didn't seem to matter either way though because they continued to shovel dirt onto the scared couple.

After filling the hole, Alan and Michael put the shovels back into the trunk of the Lincoln and drove it up the road to where Tiffany and Bruce were waiting with the Mazda. The four of them drove to

Sanderson, Florida, where they abandoned the Lincoln after wiping it clean of fingerprints. They then drove back to Jacksonville where they immediately went to an ATM and withdrew money from the Sumner's account, before retiring to a hotel. Alan and Tiffany went to another Wal-Mart where they purchased more latex gloves as well as bleach. They returned to the Sumner's home in order to clean up any evidence. They also stole a computer. Bruce stayed with the group for another day and then went home, but Alan remained with Michael and Tiffany who returned to South Carolina, where Tiffany rented two hotel rooms; one for herself and Michael and one for Alan. It should be noted that after returning home, Bruce went to a party with a plastic bag filled with different medications. At one point he announced that he had found a new job murdering people. He stated that he had buried people alive and killed them without mentioning the involvement of anyone else.

On the morning of July 10th, Carol's daughter, Rhonda, decided to report to police the fact that she hadn't been able to get hold of her mother for a few days. Since they kept in touch on a regular basis and spoke every couple days, it was highly unusual for her mother to not return her calls. The next day, the Jacksonville Sheriff's Office (JSO) went to the Sumner's home. The back door of the house was unlocked and in the kitchen there dirty after-dinner plates, which was also highly unusual for the couple. The JSO began to investigate the financial accounts of the couple and they found that large amounts of money had been withdrawn within a short time frame. Video footage from the ATM machines that the group had used showed Michael's face and the silver Mazda in the background. On July 12th, after Rhonda made a plea on local TV networks for the safe return of her parents, the Sheriff's office received a phone call from someone posing as Reggie Sumner. Dispatch contacted Detective David Meacham of the Sheriff's office and put the caller through.

Meacham: Where are you at?

Michael: We're in Delaware right now

Meacham: And what city is that in?

Michael: It's in Corpus

Meacham: Corpus, Delaware?

Michael: Yes

However, the town of Corpus, Delaware does not exist. Next, Tiffany came on the phone posing as Carol.

Meacham: Is this Carol?

Tiffany: Yes, sir, it is.

Meacham: Okay. This is Detective Meacham from the Sheriff's office. How are you doing tonight?

Tiffany: I was sleeping

Meacham: I understand. I understand you have some health problems

Tiffany: Mmhmm

Meacham: Okay. Any other problems?

Tiffany: I'm really tired right now

Meacham: What kind of problems do you have?

Tiffany: Cancer

Meacham: Cancer?

Tiffany: Mmhmm

The detective called Rhonda into the station so that she could listen to the taped conversation. She confirmed that the people posing as the Sumners were definitely not Carol and Reggie. The main reason for the call was to ensure everyone that the Sumners were alive and well and because the bank accounts had been frozen. They asked the detectives to reinstate the accounts, which they did so that they could track the money in order to locate the perpetrators. They also had the phone number from which Michael had called. Using this information, they were able to find that the phone was registered to Michael and that a call had been placed to a car rental agency in Charleston. They also learned that the cell had been used near the Sumner's home the night of the murders. Detective Meacham contacted the rental company and was told that the car had been rented to a Tiffany Cole and that it was overdue. Using the rental car's GPS system, they were able to find that the car had also been near the Sumner's residence during the time of the abduction. Using the cell phone trace, the car's GPS and the photos of Michael at different ATMs, police were able to locate the general whereabouts of the three murderers. On July 14th, with help from Tiffany's brother, who was on probation and threatened with jail, police raided a Best Western hotel in Charleston and arrested Tiffany Cole, Alan Wade, and Michael Jackson. Bruce Nixon was also picked up at his home in Florida.

While Tiffany, Michael, and Alan refused to cooperate with law enforcement, Bruce appeared to have some semblance of a conscience because he broke down and admitted to the crimes right away. He also agreed to lead police to the burial site. For the first time in TV history, documentary footage showed Bruce and detectives at the grave site where Bruce broke down in sobs. Excavation of the site began the next day. The victims were found fully clothed in a crouching position. Reggie had somehow broken his tape and was holding Carol's hand. There was two feet of dirt over their heads. With ten years of homicide under his belt, Detective Meacham said it was one of the saddest and most horrible things he had ever seen. The medical examiner determined that both Reggie and Carol were alive in the hole before they were buried. Their nostrils, mouths, throats, esophagi, and trachea had fine sprays of dirt in them, which indicated that they had inhaled it. They died from mechanical asphyxiation and smothering, caused by the dirt covering their heads while compressing their chests. She said it was the worst case of asphyxiation she'd ever seen. It was "horrendous."

At some point while in jail, but unaware that Bruce had come clean, Michael's grandmother called him.

Grandma: Michael, listen to me and don't say a word. You're in the newspaper. All over the newspaper yesterday and today

Michael: For what?

Grandma: Murder

Michael: What?!

Grandma: Murder. 'Bodies ID'd as former South Carolina couple James and Carol Sumner. Bail was denied for 18-year-old Bruce Nixon of Florida who was arrested and charged with murder, home invasion, robbery, and kidnapping.' He took them to the grave site and everything

Michael: Oh my God. Are you kidding me?

Grandma: It's right here in today's paper

Michael: Bruce took them to the f*****g spot. The f****r showed them where the spot was at?

Grandma: Yes, dear

Michael: *starts panting* Bruce just killed us all

Bruce Nixon told detectives everything that had happened and agreed to testify on behalf of the prosecution. He wasn't sentenced until after he testified against the other three group members, but in the end, he received 45 years for each victim, currently being served concurrently at Century Correctional Institution in Florida. Alan Wade was tried first.

Michael Jackson was the first to be tried. Testifying on his own behalf, Michael stated that the plan was only to rob the Sumners and that it was not going to involve murder. He said that Alan and Bruce went into the house and when they came out they drove off in the Lincoln which he then followed. He claims he had no idea that Reggie and Carol were in the trunk. According to Michael, when they arrived at the hole in Georgia, it was Alan and Bruce who told him where to park and to bring them a flashlight. It was when he arrived at the burial site that he heard Carol moan. He then stated that he questioned what the other two were doing before returning to the Mazda to wait. He did admit to impersonating Reggie. Bruce testified that Michael had been the ringleader and was the one who orchestrated everything.

After stepping down from the witness stand, Carol's daughter, Rhonda, said of Bruce, "I just wanted to hug him. He is a murderer, but in the end, he did the right thing." It was that testimony that she believed sealed Michael's fate because he was found guilty of first degree murder, robbery, and kid-napping, and sentenced to death for each murder. He is currently on death row in Florida.

Alan was next to be tried. Two witnesses who were not identified gave victim impact statements during the penalty phase. Alan's lawyer then called six of their own witnesses to testify including Bruce Nixon, Alan's mom and sister, the mother of a friend, his middle school principal, and his youth pastor. Overall, the witnesses testified that Alan's parents divorced when he was eight and his father disappeared from his life. His mother took him to church regularly and as a kid, he was kind, smart, and well-behaved. After the divorce, his mother was unable to spend a lot of time with him because she had to work a lot to support them. When he was in his teens, his mother had a bout with breast cancer. By his early teens, he began to use drugs. In the sixth grade, he was involuntarily committed to a 72-hour hold because of a drug related incident. When he was sixteen, his mom had to take him out of school or be arrested for his truancy. The next year, his mother kicked him out of the house in an attempt at tough love because his drug use was becoming worse. In 2004 Alan introduced her to Michael, whom she immediately saw as a bad influence on him. Since his arrest and before his trial, Alan had apparently become a model prisoner, obtained his G.E.D and tutored other inmates in math. Nothing seemed to sway the jury, however, because he was found guilty on all counts and voted eleven-to-one to receive the death penalty. He is also currently on death row in Florida.

Tiffany was the last to be tried. Her lawyer argued that she wasn't a major participant in the crimes. He said that she was under the control of her boyfriend Michael, and that he was the mastermind. Tiffany claimed that she believed the crime would only constitute a simple theft and that she didn't knowingly participate in the robberies, kidnapping or murders. She insisted that she did not know that Reggie and Carol were in the trunk of the Lincoln until they arrived at the burial site. The circuit judge, Michael Weatherby did not see it that way, stating that it was she who held the flashlight during the digging of the grave and was there when they were bound and placed in the trunk. He also noted that she was the one who purchased the duct tape and gloves and later pawned the jewelry and computer they had stolen. "She was thoroughly involved," Weatherby stated. "She knew exactly what she was doing and participated without hesitation." It was noted as well that she was the only one of the four who had previously known the Sumners. During the penalty phase, the prosecution called two of the victim's family members who gave impact statements. The defense attorney then called up witnesses who testified that Tiffany was of good character. Three of those witnesses were correctional officers who stated that Tiffany had been no trouble in jail and did not cause any problems. A psychiatrist, Dr. Earnest Miller, testified that she suffered from poly-substance and alcohol abuse, chronic depression, and a personality disorder. He also stated that she had witnessed abuse to family members and had been sexually abused herself by her stepfather. On the other hand, he testified that Tiffany was competent and thus he could not support a plea of insanity. Finally, he stated that she knew right from wrong and had a high average IQ. In the end, Tiffany was also found guilty of all charges and sentenced to death by a 9-3 vote. Upon hearing her fate, she bowed her head and turned to her mother, mouthing the words "I love you". Her lawyer, Quentin Till, said she had been ready for the decision. He visited her in jail that week. "I told her to be strong," he said. "...I still see her being utilized and manipulated by Michael Jackson." Revis Sumner, Reggie's brother, said that Tiffany has since written to the family, asking for forgiveness. He says he has forgiven her, but that doesn't mean she shouldn't suffer for her actions. The Reverend Jean Clark, Reggie's sister has said, "I pray for Tiffany.

I pray for all of them. I'm grieved that these four young people have wasted their lives." Chief Assistant State Attorney, Jay Plotkin, who tried all four cases said, "All of these defendants got exactly what they deserved. Justice was done." After the sentences were given and the trials were over, Reggie's son, Frederick Hallock, said, "You expect some sort of closure or some sort of good feeling when the verdict is read, but it didn't seem to help much. I just know they didn't deserve this." Currently, Tiffany is one of only five women on Florida's death row. At the time of her sentence, she was the sole woman there.

Tiffany, Michael, and Alan all filed appeals after their trials, citing multiple issues. All three were denied and their sentences were upheld. Recently, in 2015, Tiffany filed another appeal, asking for a new trial. She claims that her defense lawyers were ineffective and that she should not have been convicted of first-degree murder since she did not actually bury the bodies herself. But according to Florida law, it doesn't matter who actually committed the murder. Just knowing that it was going to happen is enough to warrant a guilty verdict. At her original trial Tiffany said, "But please remember I didn't do this. I am not the monster that created this, but I regret meeting him," referring to Michael. Upon hearing that Tiffany was asking for a new trial, Reggie's sister, Jean had this to say: "Most people are going to try to come back with something like that after the fact, because they're going to try to find a loophole and get off. But justice has a voice, and justice has to be served." And the thought of going through another trial breaks her heart. "I have family members that are still not the same and never will be the same. In fact, I don't like to involve them too much into things like this, because they can't deal with it."

In 2014, Alan Wade also filed an appeal for a new trial, citing that his lawyers did not do a good job of representing him. His appellate lawyers said that his original defense lawyers barely met with him before the trial and didn't interview witnesses prior to putting them on the stand. They also cited the lack of objections to supposedly questionable evidence. In December 2014, it was decided by the Supreme Court of Florida that his conviction be upheld.

Previous to that, Michael Jackson filed an appeal for a new trial, stating that his lawyers were also ineffective. As with Alan's trial, Michael claims that his lawyers did not make objections to certain evidence when there was clearly an objection to be made. The judge did allow an appeal hearing for his concerns and at the close of the hearing, Michael was allowed to make a statement. It went as follows:

First, I'd like to say that I am guilty of the crimes of first-degree murder, kidnapping, and robbery against Mr. and Mrs. Sumner. My reason for wanting to address the Court today is because of the many lies I told to everyone years ago at pretrial and then trial. I downplayed my involvement to look as if I were not guilty but the truth is that—the truth is that it was my idea to do this. Truly, I did not make anyone do anything. All were willing participants but I was, in fact, the leader. It was my idea to do it. I lied to this Court all throughout my trial testimony, same to [defense counsel and the State]. Even more so I lied to the people who deserve the truth the most, the family of Mr. and Mrs. Sumner, and for that, I am deeply sorry. There are no words that I could ever offer that would convey the depth of my remorse or sorrow, but again I say that I am truly sorry for what I have done and though I'm undeserving, I do ask forgiveness. My desire today is to reconcile the truth to the family of Mr. and Mrs. Sumner and to Your Honor, the attorneys and to the Court record. If necessary, I will answer any and all questions fully and truthfully. Thank you.

His conviction was upheld. Tiffany, Michael, Alan, and Bruce remain in jail today, with the former three on death row.

"It's sad," said Rhonda Alford about her parents. "It took them so long to find each other." Carol and Reggie's ashes sit in an urn in Rhonda's home, forever mixed and blended together.